THE COMPLETE GUIDE TO DACHSHUNDS

Vanessa Richie

LP Media Inc. Publishing

Text copyright © 2020 by LP Media Inc.

www.lpmedia.org

Publication Data

Vanessa Richie

The Complete Guide to Dachshunds ---- First edition.

Summary: "Successfully raising a Dachshund from puppy to old age" --- Provided by publisher.

ISBN: 978-1-952069-68-0

[1.Dachshunds--- Non-Fiction] I. Title.

Design by Sorin Rădulescu

First paperback edition, 2020

TABLE OF CONTENTS

INTRODUCTION

Go to any dog park when it is busy, and you are almost guaranteed to see at least one Dachshund, usually more than one – people who have Dachshunds usually have several. The dogs are adorable and some-what comical looking as they are so much longer than they are tall. That adorable façade actually was intentional because this is a dog that was ini-tially bred to chase animals through the brambles and woods. Dachshunds have a fairly large size range, weighing between 16 and 33 lbs. as adults. This means that, depending on the parents, you may get a small or a me-dium-sized dog. Fortunately, much of that weight goes towards the length of your dog, and not the height. This also means that you aren't going to need to buy several different crates, beds, and collars between puppyhood and adulthood.

The breed hasn't always been so small. Originating in Germany, the Dachshund was primarily a hunter, taking on wild animals such as badgers and boars. This explains not only the dogs' fearlessness, but their proclivity to barking. They weren't always so small, but when the breed was standard-ized, they were bred to be increasingly smaller, and today it is unlikely they would be able to take on a boar at their current size – not that you can ex-plain that to them.

Despite their long breeding history, Dachshunds are a fairly healthy breed. Their biggest health concern is that very distinctive long back, as it can be injured fairly easily – if you have children, you should never let them pick up your Dachshund. The dogs also tend to have dental issues, so you will not only need to plan to be diligent about taking care of their teeth, but will have to avoid activities like tug-of-war. There are plenty of other games to play with your Dachshund though. From hiding treats to tricks (if your Dachshund has the personality for it), Dachshunds love to play with their people.

Despite the fact that the breed was bred as a hunter, they are popular because of how friendly they tend to be. The fact that they are so gregari-ous can actually lead to them being the kind of small dog that gives small dogs a bad name. They do tend to be vocal, so you will have to make sure to socialize and train your Dachshund. They are intelligent, which means that training can be a mixed bag. Some of them love to please their people, while others are less enthusiastic about doing what they are told.

This is also a breed that can be very aggressive if not properly trained and socialized. They aren't dangerous like other aggressive breeds, but they do bite and this can make them a terror to both children and visitors. You will need to train children and visitors in how to interact with them, both to make sure your Dachshund isn't injured and to keep him from becoming afraid of your visitors. As long as everyone is respectful and gentle with your Dachshund, he will likely be that lovable little dog that you expected

Despite these tendencies, this is a breed that is incredibly loving and largely mellow, which is why people who have one will almost certainly always have more than one.

CHAPTER 1
A Fearless, Fun-Sized Dog

"Once you own a Dachshund, you most likely always have a Dachshund in your life. They do take longer to train, they are hard headed, but they are very loyal and have a sweetness to them only a Dachshund owner will understand."

Kim Gillet
Cameo Dachshunds

Dachshunds are easily one of the most recognizable dogs in the world. Given how long they are, those short little legs just don't match the length of the Dachshund's body. While there are other long dogs, like Corgis, Dachshunds' length seems more pronounced because of their short hair, which shows off their thin frame. It has inspired a wealth of names that define the breed's appearance. Given how friendly they are, the names are fitting because they are playful, just like a Dachshund.

There is a lot to love about this adorable little pooch.

Photo Courtesy
of Lee Roberts
Roberts Twins Photography

Photo Courtesy of Tabitha Holloman

Origins Of The Name – A Fierce Hunter

A quick look at the end of the word Dachshund makes it clear this is a breed that originated in Germany. The literal translation of Dachshund is "badger dog" because the dog was primarily a breed that hunted badgers back in the 17th century.

They were the perfect dog for what German hunters needed for chasing badgers, boar, foxes, and other larger, fierce animals because Dachshunds were independent, short, and had large chests (which meant they had greater lung capacity) and a surprising tenacity. Their low, long bodies were perfect for digging tunnels and going after animals that lived in the ground or dense brambles.

The dog's phenomenal abilities to give chase into tunnels, and being so proficient at it, seem impossible looking at a modern-day Dachshund. Today's dogs are gregarious, sweet, loving, and mellow. Watching them romp around in your home makes it nearly impossible to envision them fiercely chasing any other animal. It's an interesting duality of their nature that makes them all the more charming.

The Three Different Coat Styles And Size Variation

"There are unique personality traits associated with each coat type. Dachshunds have the MOST coat/color/pattern combinations of any dog breed!"

Elizabeth Bender
BenderDachs

Dachshunds have three very different coat styles, and there are two primary sizes of the breed. The sizes are fairly obvious; the miniature Dachshund is a small dog, while the standard size is typically heavy enough to be considered a medium-sized dog.

There are three different types of coats:

Shorthaired

This is the most common coat. Smooth and sleek, it's appropriately called a smooth coat. The dog is typically black and brown, similar to the colors of a Rottweiler.

Shorthaired Dachshund

14

Longhaired

Less common, longhaired Dachshunds are thought to have been a result of mixing the shorthaired Dachshund with the longer-haired Stoberhund. The hair is soft and needs frequent grooming as the breed is low to the ground, near dirt and debris.

Longhaired Dachshund

Wirehaired

Thought to have existed by the beginning of the 19th century, wirehaired Dachshunds were not intentionally bred until the end of that century. Breeders established the standard for the breed by breeding the shorthaired Dachshund with the German wirehaired Pinscher and Dandie Dinmont Terrier.

The different coats are ideal for different hunting conditions. Chapter 2 details the differences between these types of coats, and Chapter 14 discusses how much maintenance they each require. However, to help

Wirehaired Dachshund

your decision-making process when it comes to choosing a pup, longhaired Dachshunds will require more grooming than the other two. Thus, if you don't want to brush your pup every day, you should go with either the shorthaired or wirehaired Dachshund.

Size Standardization

FUN FACT
German Roots

Dachshunds originated in Germany nearly 300 years ago as hunting dogs. "Badger dogs" were bred for digging, tunneling, and fighting badgers. Doxies come in three coat varieties: smooth (short-haired), long-haired, and wirehaired. They also come in standard and miniature sizes.

It can be difficult to tell the difference between the two sizes (the miniature is usually around 11 pounds, while the standard starts at around 16 pounds). Unlike a lot of miniature breeds that are usually a result of pet owners wanting smaller dogs, the two Dachshund sizes are based on the type of prey they were meant to hunt. The standard breed went after larger animals, like badgers, while miniature Dachshunds chased foxes and hares.

A Symbol Of German Heritage

It is thought that the original breed from which the Dachshund evolved came from Egypt, but the breed that we know today definitely came out of Germany. The earliest Dachshunds were likely bred during the 16th century, a mix of the Braque and Pinscher, though some think that the early dogs were also cross-bred with the French Basset Hound. By the 1700s, the breed was already looking and acting in a way that is quite similar to the breed today. Their tenacious, fearless cunning was a valued trait. They could go into tunnels that breeds like the Rottweiler, German Shepherd, and Weimaraner couldn't enter. As difficult as it is to imagine today, by getting a small pack of Dachshunds together, hunters could even go after wild boar.

Despite being short, they were quick, so when they saw prey, the Dachshunds would give chase and leave the hunters behind as they chased the quarry back to their holes. Barking was incredibly important for the breed because they would go into holes after smaller animals, often disappearing into the ground without the hunters actually seeing where they went. Once they had successfully taken down their prey, the Dachshund would emerge and begin barking to let the hunter know where they were.

For more than a century, Dachshunds were a German treasure, largely becoming pets and companions. During the 1800s, they became increasingly more popular as a home companion than a hunting dog. Dogs with friendly dispositions were bred to make more of these charming little dogs, and that is why they tend to be so gregarious today. However, they still retain much of the intelligence, tenacity, and bark that were so important during earlier times.

Photo Courtesy of Esther Gorbey

While preparing for the 1972 Olympics that were held in Munich, the Germans chose a Dachshund called Waldi to serve as their mascot during the games. In honor of this little mascot, the Olympic officials chose to create the marathon route for the Olympians in the shape of a Dachshund.

A Popular Breed Around The World

During the 1800s, the popularity of the breed within Germany saw royalty adopting Dachshunds. Royalty from other nations began to notice the cute little dog, and sought to adopt some of their own. Dachshunds were a favorite of Queen Victoria, which made it easy for people from around the world to learn of the unique German dog.

By the end of the 19th century, the breed made its way to the US, where it was officially recognized in 1885. This was followed by the founding of several organizations dedicated to the friendly breed, such as the German Dachshund Club and the Dachshund Club of America. The breed's popularity continued to grow until the beginning of World War I when its ties to Germany led to people not wanting to adopt a breed that was associated with the Allies' enemies. Because of the decline in their popularity during WWI, the American Kennel Club tried to rebrand Dachshunds either as badger dogs (simply a direct translation) or as liberty pups to appeal to patriotism. This effort was stopped once the war ended.

A similar problem in popularity occurred during World War II, but it wasn't as sharp a decline as during World War I. Unlike the German

Shepherd and Rottweiler though, people did not vilify the Dachshund once World War II was over, and the breed began to makes its way into the group of most popular breeds around the world. They have been among the most common household dogs since the 1950s, and have remained there pretty much ever since.

Some places in Europe still use the breed for hunting. This has helped some Dachshunds to retain the more aggressive aspects of the breed, but those dogs are frequently bred for hunting, not for homes.

Dachshunds have become immensely popular around the world, and are celebrated in many nations. Perhaps one of the cutest ways that they are celebrated started in Australia sometime during the 1970s when it was decided to have Dachshund races. They may be fast for their very small stature, but they are certainly not racing dogs. With their paws moving as fast as possible and their ears flapping in the air, they are adorable to watch as they run. Similar races are held all over the world today.

*Photo Courtesy
of Mavourneen Smith*

Photo Courtesy
of Deborah Clark

So Many Names

The gregarious little Dachshund has acquired a wealth of nicknames, probably because being Germanic, the official breed name can be a bit more difficult to say, as well as being about as long as the dog.

Here are just a few of the nicknames this dog has been given:

- Doxie
- Doxin
- Sausage dog
- Dachie
- Dotson
- Wiener dog

And that isn't even a full list. If you end up getting a Dachshund, you will almost certainly come across many other names, and you can pick whichever one you like when talking about your little cutie. It's a very unique aspect of this breed – they attract nicknames unlike any other breed, so be prepared to learn a lot of different names to avoid confusion.

CHAPTER 2
Don't Be Fooled By Those Adorable Eyes And Stature

The Dachshund looks like a dog that needs protection. Those large eyes, low body, and droopy ears will fool anyone into thinking that the dog is helpless. Now that you know its history though, you know that this is not a breed that needs protection – unless that protection is to keep the dog from trying to take on much larger dogs.

The Dachshund's small frame packs a very large personality that makes them so popular, but that doesn't mean there aren't flaws. Do take the time to consider these flaws because a couple of them may be deal breakers – particularly the difficulty the dogs tend to have in house-training and the fact that some of them are very vocal.

*Photo Courtesy
of Anh Tran*

Photo Courtesy of Brittany Prince

The Defining Physical Characteristics Of The Dachshund

Easily the most defining part of the Dachshund's appearance is their long, sleek bodies on those short, stubby little legs. They look like sausages with fur and legs. In addition, they come in a wide range of coat colors:

- Black
- Cream
- Pied
- Brindle
- Fawn
- Red
- Brown
- Isabella
- Sable

Many of these colors can be in combinations, such as black and cream or fawn and cream. With so many different colors and three standard coat lengths, this gives Dachshunds a surprising diversity in appearance. All of the coats are straight haired and the coats are all of a medium density. The three coat types provide a very distinctive look.

Photo Courtesy
of Aaron and Minette McGeehon

- The most common type of coat is the shorthaired Dachshund. When well groomed (Chapter 14), the shorthaired coat is shiny and soft. Shorthaired Dachshunds are very easy to groom, though they do shed. The hair on their ears is so smooth that the ears look leathery, and the longest hairs tend to be on their bellies around the bald areas.

- Longhaired Dachshunds have straight hair, but it looks wavy on the ears. When properly groomed (Chapter 14), their hair is silky and smooth to the touch. There tends to be more hair on their ears, tail, and on the stomach. They require the most grooming, but also are the nicest to pet since they are so soft.

- Wirehaired Dachshunds have hair that is between the other two lengths. The longish hair gives them a slightly gloomier look, particularly around the mouth and ears, something that makes them look lovable.

All Dachshunds have a very recognizable face, with those long floppy ears, long snout, and puppy-dog eyes. Their ears tend to look disproportionately long, and you may be worried that your Dachshund could accidentally step on them – don't worry, they aren't quite that long. The eyes appear to be so large in part because of how pronounced their brow is, which helps them have more expressive looks. The eyebrows give Dachshunds expressions that are easier to identify with than many other breeds.

Though their faces are long, those jaws are incredibly strong. And behind those powerful jaws is a bark that is deeper than the dog's size suggests.

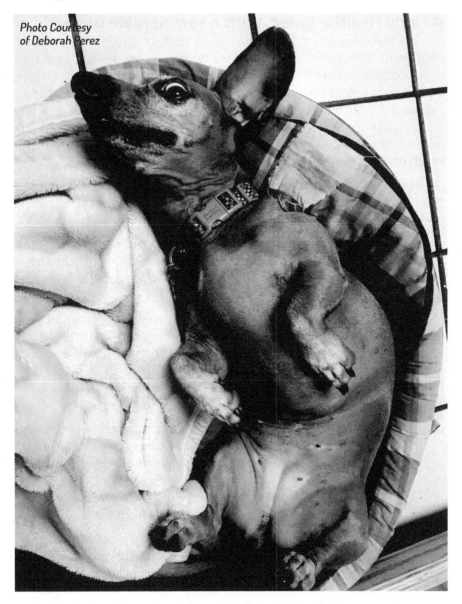

Photo Courtesy of Deborah Perez

Health Problems Common To Dachshunds

The Dachshund is a surprisingly healthy dog. The majority of potential health issues are related to their backs, but they do have a few other potential health problems that you should be aware of as you consider if this is the right breed for you to adopt.

A Fairly Healthy Breed, With A Few Notable Issues

The selective way that the dogs have been bred over the years has kept them fairly healthy, though they do have a few genetic and common problems. While this chapter discusses some of the issues, Chapter 16 provides details on what those issues are and what kind of action is required if your dog has one of them. This section is intended to help you in making your decision about adopting a Dachshund. Considering how healthy they tend to be, future health probably isn't going to be too much of a factor in your decision.

Those large eyes are prone to some issues, though not more than most aging dogs. You will want to watch for glaucoma, cataracts, and dry eyes.

Dachshunds are notorious for their dental problems. With proper care, you can likely avoid the worst complications, but you should also monitor them carefully and avoid play that could cause or exacerbate issues.

Cushing's disease isn't common, but it is a genetic problem that some Dachshunds do have. When the adrenal gland produces excessive levels of cortisone, it creates an imbalance that can make your Dachshund prone to accidents, hair loss, and an increase in appetite and weight.

FUN FACT
Know the Facts

Dachshunds are not traditionally good around strangers. They can be quite vocal, barking at anything or anyone they see. Because Doxies can be injured easily due to their size and stature, be watchful when your dog is around small children. Dachshunds can be easily stepped on, injured, and picked up incorrectly.

Dachshunds are more likely than most breeds to contract the genetic liver disease portosystemic shunt. The disease prevents the effective removal of toxins from the bloodstream.

Given their size and love of eating, Dachshunds frequently end up on the list of 10 dog breeds that are at the highest risk of obesity. You will need to be vigilant about how much your dog eats and exercises as obesity will contribute to back problems and some of the other problems associated with the breed, such as diabetes.

Dachshunds may also have stomach troubles, with Gastric Dilatation and Volvulus (GDV) being the most dangerous. This condition can be lethal. Most stomach issues are not dangerous, but could result in a lot of gas, something that will be noticeable when your dog is sitting in your lap at the end of the day.

Degenerative mitral valve disease is a problem associated with Dachshunds. The problem involves the heart valve leaking, and it usually begins when a dog is between 8 and 10 years old. Your Dachshund should be monitored for it as he reaches the golden years.

Dachshunds have several neurologic disorders including epilepsy, narcolepsy, and Lafora disease. These kinds of problems are more prominent for wirehaired Dachshunds. Symptoms of neurological disorders include excessive or spontaneous sleeping, jerking motions, tremors and seizures, and weakness or lack of balance.

A Warning About That Long Back

One of the breed's most defining characteristics is that the back is so much longer than a Dachshund is tall – it is adorable, but you also need to be careful. It is easy to hurt their backs, and you should always keep your dog on the floor – this is something that is true of all dogs, but it is even more important with dogs that have elongated backs. The following are some potential back problems:

- Intervertebral disc disease

- Spinal injuries

Because most of their back issues are related to activities, and not genetics, there are things that you will need to do to make sure your Dachshund does not hurt his back. Chapter 5 provides some of the steps you should take to prepare your home; Chapter 16 details the kinds of back problems your dog can develop which you should monitor for.

It is important to be careful because an estimated 25% of all Dachshunds will have back problems. And unlike people, they aren't able to explain their problems to you.

Intelligent, Independent, And Energetic – But Might Be Wary Of Children

"Dachshunds are extremely loyal. They love the people and other dogs in their family unit. Don't be surprised if they follow you from room to room just to be near you."

Elizabeth Bender
BenderDachs

Despite their size, this is a fearless dog that is smart enough to know how to get what he wants. That intellect can get Dachshunds in trouble, especially as they can be surprisingly stubborn. Since they were bred to chase other animals down holes, they can be incredibly mischievous if left alone in the backyard. That and their size are significant reasons why you should never leave your Dachshund alone outside.

The fact that so many of them are fearless seems completely contrary to their appearance. It is definitely a consideration if you already have pets. They are friendly, but you still need to find the time to make sure that your Dachshund is socialized. They can be wary around children. Older Dachshunds are more likely to prefer other pets in the home than children.

They can be possessive, which you will want to watch for, especially if you adopt an adult. When properly trained, the dogs can learn to share.

Despite their intelligence, they are not easy dogs to housetrain. If you don't want a dog that will take longer to potty train, you will want to find a different breed.

The other major potential problem is aggression. Given their history, Dachshunds aren't known for backing down and can lash out when they feel threatened, are afraid, or have been hurt. Chapter 7 goes into more detail about dealing with this, but it is definitely an important consideration. As difficult as it may be to believe with such a well-reputed, adorable dog, Dachshunds require socialization and training to make them the ideal dogs.

Photo Courtesy of Samantha Oakes

A Fantastic Dog For An Urban Home – Just Beware Of Barking

Dachshunds' little size makes them perfect for any home; however, you will need to have a place that is easy for them to get around in without you picking them up. Barking is a part of their breeding because it was important in the early days, so they are naturally a vocal breed. Unlike housetraining through, you may not find it too difficult to train your Dachshund to bark for a reason instead of because of boredom or small sounds. With the right training, they can be great alarm dogs.

CHAPTER 3
Finding Your Dachshund

Dachshunds are an incredibly popular breed because of how much fun they can be to have around, and their small size means they can fit into nearly any environment. They do have their faults, but if you have reached this point, you have likely decided that you can deal with those issues to have a loving, friendly dog in your home. They make great companions, but you should plan to train them, whether you adopt an adult or a puppy.

Considerations And Steps To Rescue An Adult Dachshund

How much work can you manage? Will you be able to deal with an excitable puppy that has everything to learn? Or do you prefer to work with an adult that may have problems that you have to help the dog work through? Puppies are almost always more work, but you never know what kind of experience an adult dog has been through which will affect how he reacts to the world around him.

Photo Courtesy of Dawn Berger

The hunt to find your newest family member is going to take a while, even if you decide to rescue an adult. Because of Dachshunds' fragile backs, you will need to spend time fixing up your home to help your new little friend get around if you have stairs or if you are going to allow him on the furniture. There can also be problems that result from improper breeding or the care given at the beginning of a Dachshund's life. To ensure that you get a healthy puppy that will be your loving companion for as

28

long as possible, you'll need to find a reputable breeder who cares more about the puppies than money.

The approach to adopting an adult Dachshund is the same as it is for adopting a puppy from a breeder. However, with such an intelligent dog, you will want to ask a lot more questions about adopting an adult, particularly about the dog's previous experiences.

Considerations

Rescuing any dog comes with some inherent risks. While it is possible to find Dachshund puppies at dog rescue groups, it is much more likely that you will find a rescued adult. Adopting an older Dachshund could require a lot of work, and knowing the dog's history is incredibly important so you know what to expect. Since the dogs can be stubborn, people may give up on a Dachshund without putting much effort into it.

Think about the following to determine if an adult Dachshund is a good fit for your home.

- **Why do you want to bring an adult into your home? What are your expectations for the dog?**

Dachshunds understand the commands you are giving, but they may be particularly stubborn if they haven't been properly trained.

- **Do you have the patience to work through the issues that an adult may have?**

Rescue organizations collect as much information as they can about the dogs they rescue, but their knowledge of a dog's history is usually very limited. The benefits of rescuing a Dachshund are very similar to adopting any rescue dog. You need to know about their temperament so you can start planning how to help the dog to overcome past experiences and how to resolve the issues. The odds are very good that you aren't going to be starting from scratch with housetraining. Adult dogs are awake more often than puppies and, while it may take them a bit longer to warm up to you, you can bond much faster with an adult, depending on their age.

Adult Dachshunds may be a bit more wary, especially if they were not socialized or were previously treated poorly, but that loving disposition will likely come out fairly quickly once they start to feel safe and at home. They are more likely to be wary of children if they haven't been around them before as children pose a unique threat. Once your adult dog bonds with you and your family though, it will be like flipping an af-

Photo Courtesy of Alisa Ruiz

fection switch, and then you really could not ask for a more loving and intelligent canine.

- **Are you able to pro perly dog proof your home before the dog arrives?**

You can't simply bring an adult dog into your home and let him run around unchecked. One thing that is similar to preparing your home for puppies is that you will want to dog proof your home for a rescued adult before the dog arrives. Most people think it isn't necessary to prepare their home for an adult dog. However, like with a puppy, you will need to have a dedicated space for your new dog to make sure he learns the rules before being allowed to roam the home. In the beginning you will need a space for the dog to get familiar with you and your home as you assess your new dog's personality and capabilities. It is a fairly important consideration, particularly if you have other dogs and cats, as you will want to ensure harmony in your home.

- **Do you have pets who will be affected by a new dog?**

Typically, other dogs will be the problem, but Dachshunds can still be very wary in the beginning, depending on what they've been through before coming to your home. Friendly as the dogs are, you will still want to be careful when introducing them in your home.

Good Dachshund-specific rescue organizations are cautious about adopting out a rescue with personality and socialization issues. Rescue shelters will be less careful about adopting out Dachshunds because they are popular and low risk to most homes.

You may not be able to get a complete health record for an adult Dachshund, but it is likely that you will find a dog that has already been spayed or neutered, as well as chipped. Unless you adopt a Dachshund that has health issues (these should be disclosed by the rescue organization if available), rescues tend to be less costly at the first vet visit than puppies – for the first few years it's likely you won't pay nearly as much to take care of your Dachshund's health. You will be spending a lot more time training though. Puppies have a short attention span, which equates to many short training sessions. Adults require more attention and long durations of training so that they get accustomed to listening to you. This dedicated attention is good not only for teaching the rules of the home, but for bonding with the dog.

Older dogs give you more immediate gratification. You don't have to go through the sleepless nights that come with a new puppy or the frustration of housetraining.

Finally, one of the biggest benefits of getting an adult is that they are already their full size. You don't have to guess the size your adult dog will be, making it far easier to get the right gear and dog supplies in the beginning.

Since this is a breed that is universally popular, there is an entire site dedicated to helping people who want a Dachshund to find one. If you want to rescue a Dachshund, you can start with Dachshund Station.com. They have an entire page to help you find your perfect Dachshund, including dividing up rescues by state.

You don't have to go to a rescue organization. If you want to rescue a Dachshund from a breeder, they will have a more comprehensive understanding of the dog you are rescuing. Contracts and guarantees are meant as much to protect the puppies as to protect the families who adopt them. If you want an adult, consider calling breeders to see if they have any adults available. You will need to ask them a different set of questions than if you were adopting a puppy, but they will be able to provide you with a lot of details about the dog, his personality, and if there are any potential issues.

Steps To Rescuing A Dachshund

If you are interested in looking into adopting from a rescue organization or group, there are several things to keep in mind. This section covers the questions you should ask. If you are considering adopting a puppy from a rescue group instead of a breeder, ask the same questions.

To get a better idea of the rescue organization and how much they know about the dogs they adopt out, ask the following questions.

- What was the reason the dog was surrendered?
- Did the dog have any health issues when he arrived?
- Do they know how the dog was treated by the previous family (including what kind of training the dog has had, if he was mistreated, or if he was socialized)?
- How many homes do they know the dog has been in?
- What kind of vet care has the dog had? Do they have records from before the dog arrived into their care?
- Will the dog require extra medical attention based on known or suspected problems?
- Is the dog housetrained?
- How well does the dog react to strangers and walks in familiar areas?
- Does the dog have good eating habits? Does he tend to be more aggressive when eating?
- How does the dog react to children and other pets?
- Are there any known allergies?
- Does the dog have any known additional dietary restrictions?
- Will the organization take the dog back if there are problems identified with the dog after adoption?

Rescue groups should have at least a basic understanding of how well the Dachshund interacts with other dogs as the adult dog is currently living with other dogs. For breeders, there is a benefit because the adult rescues are already living with other dogs, so they have a certain amount of socialization already completed.

Photo Courtesy
of J Hammond

Considerations For Adopting A Puppy And Picking A Breeder

Puppies are a major time investment, and a dog as intelligent and stubborn as the Dachshund will make some aspects of raising a puppy that much harder.

Think about the following to determine if a Dachshund puppy is a good fit for your home.

- **How much time do you have available? Are you willing to give up all of your free time and work your schedule around your puppy?**

One of the biggest considerations is how much time you are willing to invest. All puppies are a lot of work, starting with the moment the pup-

33

py enters your care. While the Dachshund's temperament is largely predictable, how you train and socialize your puppy will affect nearly every aspect of the dog's adult life. Training and socializing can take up a large chunk of time in the early days, but they are absolutely essential for raising a healthy Dachshund.

You also want the puppy to know that your home is safe and that everyone has the puppy's best interests in mind.

- **Are you able to be firm and consistent with such an adorable puppy?**

From the very beginning, you have to establish yourself and your family as the ones in charge so that your Dachshund understands the hierarchy from the moment he enters your home. All intelligent dogs require additional time to train because they are going to be stubborn. You will need to be prepared to be patient and consistent, no matter how frustrated you are or how cute those puppy eyes are.

- **Do you have the time, energy, and budget to puppy proof your home?**

The work to prepare your home for your puppy's arrival begins long before your puppy arrives though. Puppy proofing the home is as time-consuming as childproofing your home. If you do not have the time to puppy proof your home, then you should consider getting an adult dog. Chapter 5 provides details about the specific things you should do to prepare your home before bringing a Dachshund into it.

HELPFUL TIP
Purebred or Rescue?

How do I find a reputable Dachshund breeder? The American Kennel Club (akc.org) and The Dachshund Club of America (dachshundclubofamerica.org) have lists of reputable Dachshund breeders organized by region. When purchasing a purebred puppy, ask the breeder for the medical history of the dog's parents and grandparents. Check dachshundclubofamerica.org/rescue if you are interested in a rescue Doxie.

On the plus side, you will have more time with a puppy than with an adult. You will have records about the puppy and the puppy's parents, making it easier to identify the potential problems your Dachshund may suffer. This makes it considerably easier to ensure your puppy stays healthy and to catch potential issues earlier.

Some people find it easier to bond with puppies than with adult dogs. A young puppy will be nervous in a new home, but most adjust quickly because they are pre-disposed to enjoying the company of those around them. Your prima-ry job will be protecting your puppy and making sure that you patiently train him. We will cover this more in a later chapter.

Finding a responsible breeder is the best thing you can do for your puppy since good breeders work with only healthy parents, reducing the odds that a puppy will have serious health issues. Always take the time to research breeders. Although breeders for Dachshunds are largely reputable, that doesn't mean there won't be some who are more inter-ested in earning a lot of money than in caring for their dogs.

Choosing A Breeder

Once you understand enough about the breed to know what you are getting into, it is time to start talking to breeders. The goal is to deter-mine which breeders are willing to take the time to patiently and thor-oughly answer all of your questions. They should have as much love for their Dachshunds as they want you to feel for your new puppy. And they should want to make sure that their puppies go to good homes.

If you find someone who posts regular pictures and information about the parents and the progress of the mother's pregnancy and vet visits, that is a very good sign. The best breeders will not only talk about their dogs and the plans for the parents in the future, they will stay in contact with you after you take the puppy home and answer any ques-tions as they arise. These are the kinds of breeders who are likely to have waiting lists. The active interest in knowing about what happens to the puppies later shows that they care a great deal about each individual dog. You also want to find a breeder who is willing to talk about the po-tential problems with Dachshunds. Good breeders will want to ensure the family adopting one of their puppies is capable of properly socializ-ing and training a Dachshund. Both of these activities are essential as a puppy matures.

It is likely that for each breeder you call the conversation will last about an hour. If a breeder does not have time to talk and isn't willing to talk with you later, you can cross them off your list. After you have talked with each possible breeder, compare answers.

The following are some questions to ask. Make sure you take careful notes while interviewing the breeders:

- Ask if you can visit in person. The answer should always be yes, and if it isn't, you don't need to ask anything further. Thank the breeder and hang up. Even if the breeder is located in a different state, they should allow you to visit the facility.

- Ask about the required health tests and certifications they have for their puppies. These points are detailed further in the next section, so make sure to check off the available tests and certifications for each breeder. If they don't have all of the tests and certifications, you may want to remove the breeder from consideration.

- Make sure that the breeder always takes care of all of the initial health requirements in the first few weeks through the early months, particularly shots. Puppies require that certain procedures be done before they leave their mother to ensure they are healthy. Vaccinations and worming typically start around six weeks after the puppies are born, then need to be continued every three weeks. By the time your puppy is old enough to come home, he should be well into the procedures, or even completely through with the first phases of these important health care needs.

- Ask if the puppy is required to be spayed or neutered before reaching a certain age of maturity. Typically, these procedures are done in the puppies' best interest.

- Find out if the breeder is part of a Dachshund organization or group.

- Ask about the first phases of your puppy's life, such as how the breeder plans to care for the puppy during those first few months. They should be able to provide a lot of detail, and they should do this without sounding as though they are irritated that you want to know. They should also let you know how much training you can expect to be done prior to the puppy's arrival in your home. It is possible that the breeder may start housetraining the puppy. If so, ask how quickly the puppy has picked up on the training. You want to be able to pick up from where the breeder left off once your Dachshund reaches your home.

- See what kind of advice the breeder gives about raising your Dachshund puppy. They should be more than happy to help guide you to doing what is best for your dog because they will want the puppies to live happy, healthy lives. You should also be able to rely on a breeder's recommendations, advice, and additional care after the puppy arrives at your home. Basically, you are getting customer support, as well as a great chance of having a healthy dog.

- Ask how many breeds the breeder manages a year. How many sets of parents does the breeder have? Puppies can take a lot of time and attention, and the mother should have some downtime between pregnancies. Learn about the breeder's standard operations to find out if they are taking care of the parents and treating them like valuable family members and not strictly as a way to make money.

- Ask about aggression in the parents. Also find out if they have other dog breeds in the home. While puppies are more temperamentally malleable than adults, if they have already had some exposure to other breeds, it may make it easier to integrate them into a home that already has dogs.

Contracts And Guarantees

Breeder contracts and guarantees are meant to protect the puppies as much as they are meant to protect you. If a breeder has a contract that must be signed, make sure that you read through it completely and are willing to meet all of the requirements prior to signing it. The contracts tend to be fairly easy to understand and comply with, but you should be aware of all the facts before you agree to anything. Beyond putting down the money for the puppy, signing the contract says that you are serious about how you plan to take care of the puppy to the best of your abilities by meeting the minimum requirements set forth by the breeder. A contract may also say that the breeder will retain the puppy's original registration papers, although you can get a copy of them.

When a family does not live up to the agreement from the contract, the breeder is able to take the puppy from that family. These are the dogs that some breeders have available for adoption.

The guarantee states what health conditions the breeder promises for their puppies. This typically includes details about the dog's health and recommendations on the next steps of the puppy's care once it leaves the breeder's facility. Guarantees may also provide schedules to ensure that the health care started by the breeder is continued by the new puppy parent. In the event that a major health concern is found, the puppy will need to be returned to the breeder. The contract will also explain what is not guaranteed. The guarantee tends to be very long (sometimes longer than the contract), and you should read it thoroughly before you sign it.

Dachshund contracts usually come with a requirement to have the dog spayed or neutered once it reaches maturity (typically six months).

The contract may also contain naming requirements, health details, and a stipulation for what will happen if you can no longer take care of the animal (the dog usually goes back to the breeder). It could also include information on what will happen if you are negligent or abusive to your dog.

Health Tests And Certifications

A healthy puppy requires healthy parents and a clean genetic history. A good breeder keeps extensive records of each puppy and the parents. You will want to review each of the parents' complete history to understand what traits your puppy is likely to inherit. Pay attention to learning abilities, temperament, clinginess, and any personality trait you consider important. You can either request that documents be sent electronically to you or get them when you visit the breeder in person.

It could take a while to review the breeder's information about each parent, but it is always well worth the time you spend studying and planning. The more you know about the parents, the better prepared you will be for your puppy.

When looking for a Dachshund to adopt, there are several health concerns that you should ask breeders or rescue groups about.

The following are health tests all breeders should ensure their Dachshunds undergo:

- Cardiac Exam
- Eye examination by someone who is a member of the ACVO Ophthalmologist (they should be registered with either the OFA or the CERF)
- Patella Evaluation

Breeders who take the time to join one of the many Dachshund organizations prove that they are serious about the health of their puppies. This organization requires that a standardized set of requirements be met, so membership denotes that the breeders who join are reliable and reputable.

Selecting A Puppy From A Breeder

"If choosing a puppy from a breeder, make sure you know the personality of the parents. This will tell you a lot about what personality the puppy will have. If possible, meet the parents yourself."

Kim Gillet
Cameo Dachshunds

Selecting your puppy should be done in person. However, you can start checking out your puppy after birth if the breeder is willing to share videos and pictures. Once you are allowed to see the puppies in person, consider the following:

- Assess the group of puppies as a whole. If most or all of the puppies are aggressive or fearful, this is an indication of a problem with the litter or (more likely) the breeder. Here are a few red flags if they are displayed by a majority of the puppies:

  - Tucked tails

  - Shrinking away from people

  - Whimpering when people get close

  - Constant attacking of your hands or feet (beyond pouncing)

- Notice how well each puppy plays with the others. This is a great indicator of just how well your puppy will react to any pets you already have at home.

- Notice which puppies greet you first, and which ones hang back to observe.

- The puppies should not be fat or underweight. A swollen stomach is generally a sign of worms or other health problems.

- Puppies should have straight, sturdy legs. Splayed legs can be a sign that there is something wrong.

- Examine the puppy's ears for mites, which will cause discharge. The inside of the ear should be pink, not red or inflamed.

- The eyes should be clear and bright.

- Check the puppy's mouth for pink, healthy-looking gums.

- Pet the puppy to check his coat for the following:

  - Ensure that the coat feels thick and full. If the breeder has allowed the fur to get matted or really dirty, it is an indication that they likely are not taking proper care of the animals.

- Check for fleas and mites by running your hand from the head to the tail, then under the tail (fleas are more likely to hide under most dogs' tails). Mites may look like dandruff.

- Check the puppy's rump for redness and sores and see if you can check the last bowel movement to ensure it is firm.

Pick the puppy that exhibits the personality traits that you want in your dog. If you want a forward, friendly, excitable dog, the first puppy to greet you may be the one you seek. If you want a dog that will think things through and let others get more attention, look for a puppy that sits back and observes you before approaching.

CHAPTER 4
Preparing Your Family

Getting your family ready for your little Dachshund with a large personality is going to be a unique challenge. Their small stature, higher energy levels, and intelligence make them incredibly interesting to have around, and they tend to make themselves a part of the family much faster than you may expect. It is so funny to watch such a small, somewhat comical-looking dog be so fearless. Dachshunds are inquisitive, which can make it easy to forget that you have to be very careful with them.

As noted earlier—and it's important enough to bear repeating—it is vital that you impress upon the family that they need to be careful with the dog's back. Children in particular will need to hear this often. The little Dachshund looks cute and cuddly, which makes people want to pick them up and hold them. You and your family really have to resist this urge to keep from hurting the dog's back. Other chapters will go into the health risks, but, for now, make sure that everyone in the family understands that they should be careful with how they interact with the little one (especially younger children).

Beyond that, you will have a good number of tasks that need to be done before your new dog arrives. You must determine who will be responsible for the different needs of the dog, as well as determining where your new dog will be for at least the first couple of weeks (even an adult dog will want to have a dedicated space in the beginning as you get to know each other). You will need to establish who is the primary person responsible for the dog's care, and make sure all of the members of your family keep this in mind. That is just one of the first rules that you must make sure is in place before your Dachshund arrives.

HELPFUL TIP
Be Financially Prepared

Because Dachshund puppies range in price from $200-$3,500 depending on the quality, characteristics, and bloodline of the parents, know what you are looking for before you buy. Certain coat types, sizes, and colors will cost more because they are in demand. If you would rather adopt a Doxie, plan on spending approximately $200 to cover the costs.

Planning The First Year's Budget

Caring for a puppy is a lot more expensive than you would think. You will want to have a budget, which is a good reason to start purchasing supplies a few months in advance. When you buy the items you need, you will begin to see exactly how much you will spend a month. Of course there are some items that are one-time purchases, but many other items will have to be purchased regularly, like food and treats.

Begin budgeting the day you decide to get your puppy. The cost will include the adoption fee, which is typically higher for a purebred dog than for a rescue dog.

The vet and other healthcare costs, such as regular vaccinations and an annual checkup, should be included in your budget.

The following table can help you start to plan your budget. Keep in mind that the prices are rough averages, and may be significantly different based on where you live.

Photo Courtesy of Veronica Malhiot

Item	Considerations	Estimated Costs
Crate	This should be a comfortable space where the puppy will sleep and rest.	Wire crates:Range $60 to $350 Portable crate:Range $35 to $200
Bed	This will be placed in the crate.	$10 to $55
Leash	It should be short in the beginning because you need to be able to keep your puppy from getting overexcited and running to the end of a long line.	Short leash: $6 to $15 Retractable: $8 to $25
Doggie bags for walks	If you walk at parks, this won't be necessary. For those who don't have daily access to bags, it is best to purchase packs to ensure you don't run out.	Singles cost less than $1 each. Packs: $4 to $16
Collar	This should fit comfortably without being too loose or tight. It can be difficult to get it right at first, and you will need to adjust it as your puppy grows.	$10 to $30
Tags	These will likely be provided by your vet. Find out what information the vet provides on tags, then purchase any tags that are not provided. At a minimum, your Dachshund should have tags with your address on it in case the pup escapes.	Contact your vet before purchasing to see if the required rabies tags include your contact info.
Puppy food	This will depend on if you make your Dachshund's food, if you purchase food, or both. The larger the bag, the higher the cost, but the fewer times you will need to purchase food. You will need to purchase puppy-specific food in the beginning, but will stop after the second year. Adult dog food is more expensive, so you will need to plan for an increase in cost once your puppy reaches adulthood.	$9 to $90 per bag

Water and food bowls	These will need to be kept in the puppy's designated area. If you have other dogs, you will need separate food bowls for the puppy. If your puppy proves to be an avid chewer, consider getting a stainless steel bowl.	$10 to $40
Toothbrush/ Toothpaste	You will need to brush his teeth regularly, so plan to buy more than one toothbrush during the first year.	$2.50 to $14
Brush	Dachshund coats are fairly easy to maintain, but you should still brush them regularly. When they are puppies, brushing offers a great way to bond.	$3.50 to $20
Toys	You definitely want to get your puppy toys, and you are going to want toys for more aggressive chewers, even if your puppy goes through them remarkably quickly. You may want to keep getting your Dachshund toys as an adult (cost of adult dog toys not included).	$2.00 Packs of toys range from $10 to $20 (easier in the long run as your pup will chew through toys quickly)
Training treats	You will need these from the beginning, and likely won't need to change the treats based on your Dachshund's age; you may need to change treats to keep your dog's interest though.	$4.50 to $15

The difference in size between the puppy and an adult in size is not substantial, so you won't need to get two different crates or other supplies. However, you will need to adjust some of the pet supplies, such as the collar.

Instructing Children

You want your pup to feel comfortable from the start, which means making sure your children are careful and gentle with the dog, whether you're planning on adopting a puppy or an adult. This is a breed that looks absolutely adorable, and some kids may try to treat the dog like a toy or stuffed animal, which could be detrimental to your Dachshund.

Photo Courtesy
of Shelly Younger

You will have to make sure your kids follow all of the rules from the beginning to ensure that your puppy feels safe, happy, and isn't accidentally injured.

Remind your kids of the following rules regularly, both before the puppy arrives and after. Older teens will probably be all right to help with the puppy, but younger teens and kids should not be left alone with the puppy for a few months. Remember that you will need to be very firm to make sure that the puppy is not hurt or frightened.

The following are the five golden rules that your children should follow from the very first interaction.

1. Always be gentle and respectful.

2. Do not disturb the puppy during mealtime.

3. Chase is an outside game.

4. The Dachshund should always remain firmly on the ground. Never pick him up. Emphasize this regularly to protect your Dachshund's spine.

5. All of your valuables should be kept well out of the puppy's reach.

Since your kids are going to ask why, here are the explanations you can give them. You can simplify them for younger kids, or to start a dialogue with teens.

Always Be Gentle And Respectful

Little Dachshund puppies are very cute and cuddly, but they are also fragile. At no time should anyone play rough with the puppy (or any adult Dachshund). It is important to be respectful of your puppy to help the dog learn to also be respectful toward people and other animals.

This rule must be applied consistently every time your children play with the puppy. Be firm if you see your children getting too excited or rough. You don't want the puppy to get overly excited either, because he might end up nipping or biting someone. If he does, it isn't his fault because he hasn't learned better yet – it is the child's fault. Make sure your children understand the possible repercussions if they get too rough.

Mealtime

Dachshunds, like nearly every breed, can be protective of their food, especially if you rescue a dog that has previously had to fend for himself. Even if you have a puppy, you don't want him to feel insecure about his food because that will teach him to be aggressive when he is eating. Save yourself, your family, and your Dachshund trouble by making sure everyone knows that eating time is your Dachshund's time alone. Similarly, teach your kids that their own mealtime is off limits to the puppy. No feeding him from the table.

Photo Courtesy of Jessica Lynch

Chase

Make sure your kids understand why a game of chase is fine outside (though you'll need to monitor it), but inside the house the game is off limits.

Running inside the home gives your Dachshund puppy the impression that your home isn't safe inside because he is being chased. And it teaches your puppy that running indoors is fine, which can be very dangerous as the dog gets older and bigger. One of the last things you want is for your adult Dachshund to go barreling through your home knocking into people because it was fine for him to run in the house when he Was A Puppy.

Paws On The Ground

This is a rule that will likely require a good bit of explaining to your children as Dachshunds look a lot like toys, especially Dachshund puppies. No one should be picking the puppy up off the ground. You may want to carry your new family member around or play with the pup like a baby, but you and your family will have to resist that urge. Kids particularly have trouble understanding since they will see the Dachshund puppy as being more like a toy than a living creature. The younger your children are, the more difficult it will be for them to understand the difference.

It is so tempting to treat the Dachshund like a baby and to try to carry him around like one, but this is incredibly uncomfortable and unhealthy for the puppy. Older kids will quickly learn that a puppy's nip or bite hurts a lot more than you would think. Those little teeth are quite sharp, and you don't want the puppy to be dropped. If your children learn never to pick up the puppy things will go a lot better. Remember, this also applies to you, so don't make things difficult by doing something you constantly tell your children not to do.

Keep Valuables Out Of Reach

Valuables are not something you want to end up in the puppy's mouth, whether it's toys, jewelry, or shoes. Your kids will be less than happy if their personal possessions are chewed up by an inquisitive puppy, so teach them to put toys, clothes, and other valuables far out of the puppy's reach.

Preparing Your Current Dogs

Dachshunds tend to be easygoing, so the interaction with your dogs is going to depend on your current dogs' personality. This means if you already have canines in your home, they are going to need to be prepared for the new arrival.

> **Here are the important tasks to do to prepare your current pets for your new arrival.**
> - Set a schedule for activities and the people who will need to participate.
> - Preserve your current dogs' favorite places and furniture, and make sure their toys and items are not in the puppy's space.
> - Have playdates at your home and analyze your dogs to see how they react to an addition.

Stick To A Schedule

Obviously, the puppy is going to get a lot of attention, so you need to make a concerted effort to let any current pets know that you still love and care for them. Make a specific time in your schedule just for your current dog or dogs, and make sure that you don't stray from that schedule after the puppy's arrival.

Make sure that you plan to have at least one adult around for each dog you have. Cats are generally less of a concern, but you will probably want to have at least one other adult around when the puppy comes home. We will go into more detail later about what the roles of the other adults will be, but, for now, when you know what date you will be bringing your puppy home, ensure that you have additional adults to help out. You may need to remind them as the time nears, so set an alert on your phone, as well as the date, time, and pickup information for your puppy.

One benefit of having a schedule for your other dogs in place before your Dachshund puppy arrives is that it will then be easy to keep a schedule with the puppy. Dachshunds love to know what to expect, at least in the beginning.

Your puppy is going to eat, sleep, and spend most of the day and night in his assigned space. This means that the space cannot block your current canine from his favorite furniture, bed, or any place where he rests over the course of the day. None of your current dog's stuff should

be in this area, and this includes toys. You don't want your dog to feel like the puppy is taking over his territory. Make sure your children understand to never to put your current dog's stuff in the puppy's area.

Your dog and the puppy will need to be kept apart in the early days, (even if they seem friendly) until your puppy is done with vaccinations. Puppies are more susceptible to illness during these days, so wait until the puppy is protected before the dogs spend time together. Leaving the puppy in the puppy space will keep them separated during this critical time.

Helping Your Dog Prepare – Extra At Home Playdates

Here are things that will best help prepare your pooch for the arrival of your puppy.

- Think about your dog's personality to help you decide the best way to prepare for that first day, week, and month. Each dog is unique, so you will need to consider your dog's personality to determine how things will go when the new dog arrives. If your current dog loves other dogs, this will probably hold true when the puppy shows up. If your dog has any territorial tendencies, you will need to be cautious about the introduction and first couple of months so that your current dog learns that the Dachshund is now a part of the pack. Excitable dogs will need special attention to keep them from getting overly agitated when a new dog comes home. You don't want them to be so excited they accidentally hurt the little Dachshund.

- Consider the times when you have had other dogs in your home and how your current dog reacted to these other furry visitors. If your canine displayed territorial tendencies, you should be extra careful with

Photo Courtesy of Karen Syler

how you introduce your new pup. If you haven't ever invited another dog to your home, have a couple of playdates with other dogs at your home before your new Dachshund puppy arrives. You have to know how your current furry babies will react to new dogs in the house so you can properly prepare. Meeting a dog at home is very different from encountering one outside the home.

● Think about your dog's interactions with other dogs for as long as you have known the pup. Has your dog shown either protective or possessive behavior, either with you or others? Food is one of the reasons dogs will display some kind of aggression because they don't want anyone trying to eat what is theirs. Some dogs can be protective of people and toys too.

The same rules apply, no matter how many dogs you have. Think about the personalities of all of them as individuals, as well as how they interact together. Just like people, you may find that when they are together your dogs act differently, which you will need to keep in mind as you plan their first introduction.

See Chapter 8 for planning to introduce your current dogs and your new puppy, and how to juggle a new puppy and your current pets.

Potentially Friendly To Your Whole Family, Even Cats

One of the reasons that so many people are so willing to bring a Dachshund into the home is that the breed seems to be perfectly loving and affectionate with everyone. Older dogs that have had a bad experience or who have not been properly socialized may not be as kind to your cats, so you will need to be more careful about the introduction. Even if the cat is larger than your new family member, your Dachshund is not going to be afraid of him. Usually though, Dachshunds tend to be easy to introduce to dogs and cats already in your home. It is more likely that your cat will be annoyed with this new interloper than your Dachshund will be interested in chasing the cat. Of course, if your cat runs, the pup is going to think it is a game, but for most Dachshunds, they just want to play.

There is some preparation you will need to make around your home (Chapter 5), and you are going to need to be careful about introducing your new Dachshund to your other pets (Chapter 7).

CHAPTER 5
Preparing Your Home And Schedule

Regardless of the age of the Dachshund you bring home, you are going to need to take a few hours to prepare your home. Since both puppies and adults are low to the ground, many of the precautions you take will be the same – you want to see all of the potential risks from the ground level. You are also going to need to do a bit extra to promote a healthy back for your long little love.

As innocent as they appear, you have to remember that Dachshunds are smart dogs, and they can figure things out that you would not expect. That means that they are going to be looking around, seeing just what they can explore. This is dangerous for both your puppy and your home. Your Dachshund is going to be curious and will try to get into cabinets, low trash cans, and other items around your home that are easily accessible. Preparing your home for a puppy small enough to get into tight spaces is definitely tricky. Keep in mind this is a breed that has cen-

Photo Courtesy of Shari Starling

*Photo Courtesy
of Chloe Reynolds & Conor Chuck*

turies of scurrying down holes, so they can weasel their way into some very tight spaces if you aren't careful.

The week before your puppy arrives, you should conduct numerous checks to ensure that your home is safe for the new family member. Making sure your new Dachshund has a safe space with all of the essentials (including toys) will make the arrival of your newest family addition a great time for everyone – especially your new canine companion.

Even if you bring an adult Dachshund home, you have to prepare for the arrival of an incredibly headstrong toddler that can get into places that you had not considered remotely possible. Dachshunds have to learn that you are in control, which means that you have to gain their respect before they will listen to you. If your dog has not already learned not to grab food, climb on furniture, or whatever other restrictions you have implemented in your home, you will have your work cut out for you when it comes to training your new friend. Dog-proofing your home will help you keep your dog safe while he is learning to listen to you.

Photo Courtesy
Erin Green

Creating A Safe Space For Your Dog Or Puppy

Your puppy will need a dedicated space that includes a crate (more information on this in the next section), food and water bowls, pee pads, and toys. All of these things will need to be in the area where the puppy will be when you are not able to give him attention. The puppy space should be safe and gated so that the puppy cannot get out, and young children and other dogs cannot get in. It should be a safe space where the puppy can see you going about your usual business and feel comfortable.

Do's And Don'ts For Keeping Your Dachshund's Back Healthy

Your Dachshund's back is easily the greatest potential health risk to your dog. Even if your canine doesn't have any genetic issues, he can hurt his back if you don't properly prepare your home. This will be even more critical for an adult as for a puppy.

Remember, you should never pick up your Dachshund. This is a significant health risk as gravity will cause their bodies to twist and contort in ways that will hurt that long back. Never pick up your Dachshund.

To ensure that you don't have any reason to pick up your puppy – something that will be especially important if you have kids – set up ramps to help your little one reach the areas your Dachshund is allowed to go. If you allow your Dachshund on the furniture, you should have a ramp for him to go up and down. Jumping off furniture can hurt him. Jumping off your bed or couch on a daily basis significantly increases the odds of back injury.

Photo Courtesy Jennifer Wyatt

You can also install small steps. If you have stairs, that is fine. Just make sure they aren't too steep to support your dog's back. If the stairs are steep, use a baby gate to keep your Dachshund from using them. This will mean that the Dachshund's area will be exclusively downstairs. If the stairs are outside, built a ramp to the side for your Dachshund.

Crates And Crate Training

Crate training a Dachshund puppy can be fairly easy (much easier than housetraining), but not if you have a crate that is too big, too small, or too hard for your dog to feel like it is a safe place. To make training easy later, you need to make sure that the puppy's crate and bedding are already set up and ready before your puppy arrives.

Never treat the crate like it is a prison for your puppy. Your Dachshund should never associate the crate with punishment – it's meant to be a safe haven after overstimulation or when it's time to sleep. Ensure your dog

Photo Courtesy
Elisabeth Linka

never associates the crate with punishment or negative emotions. The crate should be adjustable so that you can make it a bit larger when your puppy becomes an adult. You can also get your puppy a carrying crate in the early days to make trips to the vet a little easier. This crate won't work when your Dachshund is an adult (you can just walk your dog into the vet's office as an adult), but the carrying crate has plenty of space for a puppy.

As mentioned in an earlier chapter, you can use the crate to help with housetraining. While Dachshunds don't tend to be easy to house-train, you may want to have a pee pad in the puppy's area as far from the crate as possible. This will give your puppy a place to go during inclement weather. Make sure to find out from the breeder if the puppy has already begun housetraining. If the puppy is already making progress, you may not want to add the pee pad.

Purchase And Prepare Supplies And Tools

Planning for your puppy's arrival means buying a lot of supplies up front. The list is longer than most people realize, so take some time to really think about what you will need based on your home and circumstances. If you start making purchases around the time you identify the breeder you will get the puppy from, you can stretch out your expenses over a longer period of time. This will make it seem a lot less expensive than it actually is. The following are recommended items you should have purchased before bringing your new dog home:

- Crate
- Bed
- Leash
- Doggie bags for walks
- Collar
- Tags
- Puppy food/adult food (depending on age of dog)
- Water and food bowls (sharing a water bowl is usually okay, but your puppy needs his or her own food dish if you have multiple dogs)
- Toothbrush/Toothpaste
- Brush
- Toys
- Training treats
- Ramps or steps if you plan to use them

Talk to your vet before buying any medications, including flea treatments.

Photo Courtesy
of Emily Badman

Puppy-Proof The House

"Think like a pup. Lie down on the floor and see what you can get into. Look for small openings, electrical cords, dangerous spaces or items, and breakables. Put them up or secure them so your pup can't get into them. Be careful what chemicals you use to clean with because everything is going to go in their mouths. Make sure everything they can get to is safe for them to play with and chew on."

Shona Malapelli
Malapelli's Minions Miniature Dachshunds

Preparing for the arrival of a puppy is time consuming, and all of the most dangerous rooms and items in your home will be equally as dangerous to your puppy as they would be to a baby. The biggest difference is that your Dachshund is going to be mobile much faster than a child. He will potentially get into dangerous situations almost immediately if you don't eliminate all of the dangers ahead of his arrival in your home.

Be aware that puppies will try to eat virtually anything. Nothing is safe – not even your furniture. They'll gnaw on wood and metal. Anything within their reach is considered to be fair game. Keep this in mind as you go about puppy-proofing your home.

Indoor Hazards And Fixes

This section details the areas inside your home where you should focus your attention. In case of problems, have your vet's number posted on the fridge and in at least one other room in the house. If you set this up before your pup arrives, it will be there if you need it. Even if you program the vet's phone number into your phone, another family member or someone taking care of your Dachshund may still need it.

Dachshunds can get into nearly everything at their height, and they will be exploring a lot when given the opportunity. As intelligent as the breed is, it's best to overestimate what your puppy can do and prepare accordingly. Get low and see each room from your Dachshund's perspective. You are almost guaranteed to find at least one thing you missed.

Hazards	Fixes	Time Estimate
Kitchen		
Poisons	Keep in secured, childproof cabinets or on high shelves	30 min
Trash cans	Have a lockable trash can, or keep it in a secured location	10 min
Appliances	Make sure all cords are out of reach	15 min
Human Food	Keep out of reach	Constant (start making it a habit)
Floors		
Slippery surfaces	Put down rugs or special mats designed to stick to the floor	30 min – 1 hour
Training area	Train on non-slip surfaces	Constant
Bathrooms		
Toilet brush	Either have one that locks or keep out of reach	5 min/bathroom
Poisons	Keep in secured, childproof cabinets or on high shelves	15 – 30 min/ bathroom
Toilets	Keep closed Do not use automatic toilet cleaning chemicals	Constant (start making it a habit)
Cabinets	Keep locked with child-proof locks	15 – 30 min/ bathroom
Laundry Room		
Clothing	Store clean and dirty clothing off the floor, and out of reach	15 – 30 min
Poisons (bleach, pods/detergent, dryer sheets, and misc. poisons)	Keep in secured, childproofed cabinets or on high shelves	15 min
Around the Home		
Plants	Keep off the floor	45 min – 1 hour
Trash cans	Have a lockable trash can, or keep it in a secured location	30 min

Electrical cords, window blind cords	Hide them or make sure they are out of reach; pay particular attention to entertainment and computer areas	1.5 hours
Poisons	Check to make sure there aren't any in reach (WD40, window/screen cleaner, carpet cleaner, air fresheners); move all poisons to a centralized, locked location	1 hour
Windows	Check that cords are out of reach in all rooms	1 – 2 hours
Fireplaces	Store cleaning supplies and tools where the puppy can't get into them Cover the fireplace opening with something the puppy can't knock over	10 min/fireplace
Stairs	Cordon off so that your puppy can't try to go up or down them; make sure to test any puppy gates	10 – 15 min
Coffee tables/ End tables/ Nightstands	Clear of dangerous objects (e.g., scissors, sewing equipment, pens, and pencils) and all valuables	30 – 45 min

If you have a cat, keep the litter box up off the floor. It needs to be somewhere that your cat can easily get to but your Dachshund cannot. Since this involves teaching your cat to use the new area, it's something you should do well in advance of the puppy's arrival. You don't want your cat to undergo too many significant changes all at once. The puppy will be enough of a disruption – if your cat associates the change with the puppy, you may find the feline protesting by refusing to use the litter box.

Outdoor Hazards And Fixes

This section details the things outside your home that need your attention ahead of your puppy's arrival. Also post the vet's number in one of the sheltered areas in case of an emergency.

Hazards	Fixes	Time Estimate
Garage		
Poisons	Keep in secured, childproofed cabinets or on high shelves (e.g., car chemicals, cleaning supplies, paint, lawn care) – this includes fertilizer	1 hour
Trash bins	Keep them in a secured location	5 min
Tools (e.g., lawn, car, hardware, power tools)	Make sure all cords are out of reach: Keep out of reach and never hanging over the side of surfaces	30 min – 1 hour
Equipment (e.g., sports, fishing)	Keep out of reach and never hanging over the side of surfaces	Constant (start making it a habit)
Sharp implements	Keep out of reach and never hanging over the side of surfaces	30 min
Bikes	Store off the ground or in a place the Dachshund cannot get to (to keep the pup from biting the tires)	20 min
Fencing (Can Be Done Concurrently)		
Breaks	Fix any breaks in the fencing. Dachshunds are escape artists, so you need to make sure they can't easily get out of your yard.	30 min – 1 hour
Gaps	Fill any gaps, even if they are intentional, so your Dachshund doesn't escape	30 min – 1 hour
Holes/ Dips at Base	Fill any area that can be easily crawled under	1 – 2 hours
Yard		
Poisons	Don't leave any poisons in the yard	1 – 2 hours

Plants	Verify that all low plants aren't poisonous to dogs; fence off anything that is (such as grape vines)	45 min – 1 hour
Tools (e.g., lawn maintenance and gardening tools)	Make sure they are out of reach; Make sure nothing is hanging over the sides of outdoor tables	30 min – 1 hour

Never leave your Dachshund alone in the garage, even when he is an adult. It is likely that your puppy will be in the garage when you take car trips, which is why it is important to puppy-proof it.

Dachshunds were bred to dig, so you are going to need to make sure that there are no areas that already have holes if you don't want your Dachshund to make them bigger. If you have a fence, you are going to need to do a very thorough inspection to make sure there isn't anything that can be easily dug up.

Fence inspections are something you are going to need to continue to schedule at least once a month. Dachshunds are proficient diggers, which means you are going to need to see if your pup has managed to create holes. This is also why you can never leave your Dachshund outside on his own. You will always need to attend your dog when he goes out to the bathroom or to play because when he is bored, he will very likely start to dig. You don't want to put him out to use the bathroom only to find he has escaped in the five minutes you left him outside alone.

Just like with the inside, you will need to follow up your outdoor preparations by getting down low and checking out all areas from a puppy's perspective. Again, you are all but guaranteed to find at least one thing you missed.

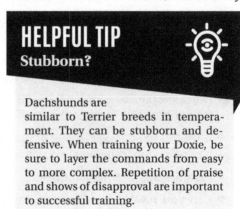

HELPFUL TIP
Stubborn?

Dachshunds are similar to Terrier breeds in temperament. They can be stubborn and defensive. When training your Doxie, be sure to layer the commands from easy to more complex. Repetition of praise and shows of disapproval are important to successful training.

Choosing Your Veterinarian

Start looking around for a vet for your Dachshund even before you choose a breeder. You should have your vet chosen before you bring your dog home. Whether you get a puppy or an adult, you should take your canine to the vet within 48 hours (24 hours is strongly recommended) of his arrival to make sure your dog is healthy. If there is a vet near you who specializes in or has worked with Dachshunds before, that will be best for your pup. Considering the Dachshund's personality, you want a vet who knows how to work with a headstrong pooch. Getting an appointment with a vet can take a while, especially one that specializes in a particular breed, just like getting a doctor's appointment. You need to have your vet and the first appointment booked well in advance of your dog's arrival.

Here are some things to consider when looking for a vet:

- What is the vet's level of familiarity with Dachshunds?
- The vet doesn't have to be a specialist; Dachshunds are a very popular breed. However, you want your vet to have some experience with them, particularly as the breed has a number of health concerns. Familiarity with the possible problems will help to identify symptoms or potential issues as early as possible.
- How far from your home is the vet?
- You don't want the vet to be more than 30 minutes away in case of an emergency.
- Is the vet available for emergencies after hours or can they recommend a vet in case of an emergency?
- Is the vet part of a local vet hospital if needed, or does the doctor refer patients to a local pet hospital?
- Is the vet the only vet or one of several partners? If he or she is part of a partnership, can you stick with just one vet for office visits?
- How are appointments booked?
- Can you have other services performed there, such as grooming and boarding?
- Is the vet accredited?
- What are the prices for the initial visit and the normal costs, such as for shots and regular visits?
- What tests and checks are performed during the initial visit?

Before bringing your dog home, make time to visit the vet you are considering so that you can look around to see what the environment is like inside the office. Ask if you can speak to the vet to see if he or she is willing to help put you at ease and answer your questions. A vet's time is valuable, but he or she should have a few minutes to help you feel confident that he/she is the right choice to help take care of your canine.

CHAPTER 6
Bringing Your Dachshund Home

That first time your Dachshund walks through the door is going to be a memorable experience to look back on over the years. Your sweet little pup is going to quickly become a part of your home, and it all starts with his arrival.

While that part is going to be incredibly memorable, there is going to be a lot that you need to keep in mind to ensure your pup starts to learn who is in charge while feeling comfortable in his new home.

Photo Courtesy of Traci Gratzek

Photo Courtesy
of Sophie Ford

You never know exactly how your puppy or adult dog will react, but you know there is going to be just as much uncertainty on his part as there is on yours. With their affable personality and curiosity, you probably aren't going to have nearly so much anxiety as with other small breeds. That curiosity is probably going to win out and your puppy will want to explore. Still, you are going to have to make sure that the exploration is done in a safe environment – no running loose around the home, not even if you bring home an adult. Do expect the adult pup to be a little more wary though as you may not know what his previous experiences were.

Make sure to read Chapter 7 about how to introduce your adult dog to a multi-pet home. While Dachshunds don't tend to be aggressive, your new dog may not have had a positive experience with other dogs in the past. You want to make sure to take it slow in the early days.

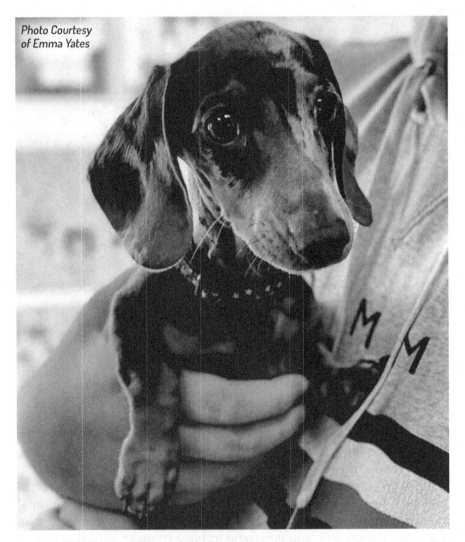

Photo Courtesy of Emma Yates

Final Preparations And Planning

Most intelligent breeds require a constant presence for the first week and as much of the first month as possible. They can figure out a way of escaping from their enclosure, so you need someone home to stop any escape attempts. You should plan to take time off from work or negotiate working from home during at least the first 24 hours, if not the first 48 hours. The best-case scenario would have you being at home for the first week or two. The more time you can dedicate to helping your new little friend become accustomed to his new surroundings in those first few days, the better for your new family member and the more quickly your pup will feel comfortable in his new environment.

The following are some useful checklists to get you through the preparation for your puppy and the aftermath of his arrival at your home.

Ensure You Have Food And Other Supplies On Hand

Do a quick check to ensure that you have everything you need. If you created a list based on the basic supplies from Chapter 5, review the list the day before your Dachshund arrives and make sure you have everything on it. Take a few moments to consider if there is anything you are missing, too. This will hopefully save you from having to try to rush out to buy additional supplies after the arrival of your new family member.

Design A Tentative Puppy Schedule

Prepare a tentative schedule to help you get started over the course of the first week. Your days are about to get very busy, so you need somewhere to start before your puppy arrives. Use the information from Setting a Schedule to get started, but make sure you do this earlier instead of later. The following are the three important areas to have established for your puppy's schedule:

- Feeding

- Training (including housetraining)

- Playing

When you bring home a puppy, you may be expecting high energy. However, puppies of any breed (no matter how active they will be later) require a lot of sleep. Expect your puppy to sleep between 18 and 20 hours per day. Having a predictable sleep schedule will help your puppy to grow up healthier.

In the beginning, you won't need to worry about making sure that your puppy is tired out by the end of the day. His stamina will build fairly quickly, though, so by the end of the first year your pup will be a lot more active. One of the best things about the breed is that they tend to have energy levels appropriate to their situation, so you aren't going to be as hard pressed to tire your Dachshund out as you would a Beagle or Jack Russell Terrier. You will still need to make sure that he gets enough exercise based on his caloric intake, because the breed is prone to obesity, which puts a lot of stress on their backs.

In the early days, your puppy's schedule will largely revolve around sleeping and eating, with some walking, and socialization. Waking hours will include training and play.

Do A Quick Final Puppy-Proofing Inspection Before The Puppy Arrives

No matter how busy you are, or how carefully you followed the puppy-proofing checklists from the previous chapter, you still need to take the time to inspect your home one more time before the puppy arrives. Set aside an hour or two to complete this a day or two before the puppy arrives.

Initial Meeting

Have a meeting with all of the family members to make sure all of the rules discussed in Chapter 4 are remembered and understood before the puppy is a distraction. This includes how to handle the puppy. Determine who is going to be responsible for primary puppy care, including who will be the primary trainer. To help teach younger children about responsibility, a parent can pair with a child to manage the puppy's care. The child can be responsible for things like keeping the water bowl filled and feeding the puppy, while a parent oversees the tasks.

Picking Up Your Puppy Or Dog And The Ride Home

Picking up your puppy takes a good bit of planning and preparation, especially if you are going to the breeder's home. If possible, plan to pick up your puppy on a weekend or at the beginning of a holiday so you can spend unrushed time at home with him. This section covers the preparation and actual trip, but not what to do if you have other dogs that you need to introduce (Chapter 8).

As tempting as it is to cuddle with your puppy, using a crate for the ride home is both safer and more comfortable for the puppy. Two adults should be present on the first trip.

- The crate should be anchored in the car for safety and include a cushion. If you have a long trip, bring food and water and plan to stop to give them to the puppy during intervals of the trip. Do not put them in the crate as they will not be anchored down, and sloshing water can scare your puppy. You can cover the bottom of the crate with a towel or pee pad in case of accidents.

- Call the breeder to make sure everything is still on schedule and make sure the puppy is ready.

- Ask, if you haven't already, if you can get the mother to leave her scent on a blanket to help make the puppy's transition more comfortable.

- Make sure your other adult remembers and will be on time to head to the pick-up destination.

- If you have other dogs, make sure that all of the adults involved know what to do, the time and where to go for that first neutral territory meeting.

If you do not have other dogs, you can pick up your puppy and head straight home. If you have a long trip (more than a couple of hours), build breaks into it every few hours to give your puppy a chance to stretch, exercise, drink, and use the bathroom. Do not leave the puppy alone in the car for any amount of time. If you have to use the restroom, at least one adult must remain with the puppy during each stop.

Ask the breeder if the puppy has been in a car before, and, if not, it is especially important to have someone who can give the puppy attention while the other person drives. The puppy will be in the crate, but someone can still provide comfort. It will definitely be scary because the puppy no longer has mom, siblings, or known people around, so having someone present to talk to the puppy will make it less of an ordeal for the little guy.

This is the time to start teaching your puppy that car trips are enjoyable. This means making sure that the crate is secure. You don't want to terri-

Photo Courtesy
of Peyton Wilhelm

73

fy the puppy by letting the crate slide around while he is sitting helpless inside it.

When you arrive home, immediately take the puppy or dog outside to use the bathroom. Even if the puppy or dog had an accident on the way, this is the time to start training your new family member where to use the bathroom.

The First Vet Visit And What To Expect

A vet's visit is necessary within the first day or two of your puppy's arrival and may be required in the contract you signed with the breeder. You need to establish a baseline for the puppy's health so that the vet can track your puppy's progress and monitor to ensure everything is going well as your Dachshund grows. The initial assessment gives you more information about your puppy, as well as giving you a chance to ask the vet questions and get advice. It also creates an important rapport between your Dachshund and the vet.

That first vet visit will be interesting and very different from subsequent visits. Your pup won't know what to expect since he hasn't been to that particular vet before. Try as best as you can to ease his anxiety. You want this first visit to set a positive tone for all future visits.

There are several things that you will need to do before the day of the appointment:

- Find out how early you need to arrive to complete the paperwork for the new patient.

- Find out if you should bring a stool sample for that first visit, too. If so, collect it the morning of the visit and make sure to take it with you.

- Bring in the paperwork provided by the breeder or rescue organization for the vet to add to your pup's or dog's records.

Upon your arrival, your puppy may want to meet the other pups and people in the office, which is something that can be encouraged as long as you keep some basic rules in mind. After all, this is a chance for you to work on socializing the puppy and to create an initial positive experience to associate with the vet, although you will need to be careful. Always ask the owner if it is all right for your puppy to meet their pet, and wait for approval before letting your puppy move forward with meeting other animals. Pets at the vet's office are very likely to not be feeling great, which means they may not be very affable. You don't want a grumpy older dog or a sick animal to nip or scare your puppy. Negative social experiences are something your puppy will remember, and will make going to the vet something to dread or resist. Nor do you want your puppy to be exposed to potential illnesses while still getting his shots.

During the first visit, the vet will conduct an initial assessment of your Dachshund. One of the most important things the vet will do is take your puppy's weight. This is something you are going to have to monitor for your Dachshund's entire life because the breed is prone to obesity. Record the weight for yourself so you can see how quickly the puppy is growing. Ask your vet what a healthy weight is at each stage, and record that as well. Dachshunds grow unbelievably fast during the first year, but you should still make sure your dog isn't gaining more weight than is healthy.

The vet will set the date for the next set of shots, which will likely happen not too long after your puppy arrives. When it is time for his vaccinations, be prepared for a day or two of your puppy feeling under the weather.

Crate And Other Preliminary Training

As mentioned, training starts from the moment your Dachshund becomes your responsibility. Considering the fact that your dog may be stubborn, you want to start getting your pup used to the idea that you are in charge. This will help play against the Dachshund's headstrong nature. Don't expect training to eliminate the behavior, but you can at least let your new pup know what the hierarchy is.

Puppies younger than six months old shouldn't be in the crate for hours at a time. They will not be able to hold their bladders that long, so you need to make sure they have a way to get out and use the restroom in an acceptable place. If you get an adult dog that is not housetrained, you will need to follow the same rules.

Make sure the door is set so that it doesn't close on your dog during his initial sniff of the crate. You don't want your Dachshund to get hit by the door as it is closing and scare him.

STEPS TO INTRODUCING YOUR PUPPY TO THEIR CRATE

1 — LET YOUR DACHSHUND SNIFF THE CRATE.
Talk to him while he does this, using a positive, happy voice. Associate the first experience in the crate with excitement and positive emotions so that your dog understands it is a good place. If you have a blanket from the puppy's mother, put it in the crate to help provide an extra sense of comfort.

2 — DROP A COUPLE OF TREATS INTO THE CRATE
if your canine seems reluctant to enter it. Do NOT force your dog into the crate. If your dog doesn't want to go all the way into this strange little space, that is perfectly fine. It has to be his decision to enter so that it isn't a negative experience.

3 — FEED YOUR DOG IN THE CRATE FOR A WEEK OR TWO.
This will help create some positive emotions with the crate, as well as helping you to keep the food away from other pets if you have them.

a.   If your dog appears comfortable with the crate, put the food all the way at the back of the crate.

b.   If not, place the food bowl in the front, then move it further back in the crate over time.

4 — START CLOSING THE DOOR
once your dog appears to be eating comfortably in the crate. When the food is gone, open the crate immediately.

5 — LEAVE THE DOOR CLOSED
for longer periods of time after your dog has eaten. If your pup begins to whine, you have left your Dachshund in the crate for too long.

6 — CRATE YOUR DOG FOR LONGER PERIODS OF TIME
once your dog shows no signs of discomfort in the crate when he is eating. You can start to train him to go into the crate by simply saying "crate" or "bed," then praise your dog to let him know that he has done a great job.

Repeat this for several weeks until your dog feels comfortable in the crate. Doing this several times each day can help your dog to learn that everything is all right and that the crate is not a punishment. Initially, you will be doing this while you are still at home or when you go out to get the mail. As soon as your puppy can make it for half an hour without whining while you're out of the room, you can start leaving your pup alone while you are gone, keeping the time to no more than an hour in the beginning.

Once your dog understands he is not supposed to tear up your home, the crate training is complete.

The focus during these first few weeks is to start housetraining and minimize any undesirable behavior. Training from the start is vital, but don't take your new puppy to any classes just yet. This is because most puppies have not had all of the necessary shots, and good trainers will not allow them in classes until the full first round of shots is complete. Chapters 10 and 12 provide a closer look at the different kinds of training you should begin and how to follow through after the first few weeks.

First Night Frights

That first night is going to be scary to your little Dachshund puppy. As understandable as this may be, there is only so much comfort you can give your new family member. Just like with a baby, the more you respond to cries and whimpering, the more you are teaching a puppy that negative behaviors will provide the desired results. You will need to be prepared for a balancing act to provide reassurance that things will be all right while keeping your puppy from learning that crying gets your attention.

Create a sleeping area just for your puppy near where you sleep. The area should have the puppy's bed tucked safely into a crate. It offers him a safe place to hide so that he can feel more comfortable in a strange new home. The entire area should be blocked off so that no one can get into it (and the puppy can't get out) during the night. It should also be close to where people sleep so that the puppy doesn't feel abandoned. If you were able to get a blanket or pillow that smells like the mother, make sure this is in your puppy's space. Consider adding a little white noise to cover unfamiliar sounds that could scare your new pet.

Photo Courtesy
of Ariel Bosin

Your puppy will make noises over the course of the night. Don't move the puppy away, even if the whimpering keeps you awake. If you give in, over time the whimpering, whining, and crying will get louder. Being moved away from people will only scare the puppy more, reinforcing the anxiety he feels. During the night, your puppy is not whimpering because he's been in the crate too long; he's scared or wants someone to be with him – he's probably never been alone at night before arriving at your home. Spare yourself some trouble later by teaching the puppy that whimpering doesn't always work to get him out of the crate. Over time, simply being close to you at night will be enough to reassure your puppy that everything will be all right.

Puppies will need to go to the bathroom every two to three hours, and you will need to get up during the night to make sure your puppy understands that he is to always go to the bathroom either outside or on the pee pad. If you let it go at night, you are going to have a difficult time training him that he cannot go in the house later, especially since Dachshunds are so hard to housetrain already.

Dachshund really shouldn't be allowed on the bed because they should not be jumping off of the furniture. However, if you do let your dog on the bed, you will need to have a ramp or stairs and your dog will need to be trained to use them to get up and down from the bed. If you choose to let your dog on the bed, wait until he is fully housetrained. You are going to need to make sure the training is out of the way, both for the housetraining and using the stairs/ramp. It is best to simply keep your Dachshund off the furniture so that your pup doesn't get hurt and to keep your furniture from being ruined.

CHAPTER 7
The Multi-Pet Household

"Never leave your new puppy alone with your current dog. Supervised play is a must. Let them get used to each other but make sure they are both safe. Puppies have very sharp teeth and may not yet know that biting too hard hurts. This can cause an older pet to react sharply."

Shona Malapelli
Malapelli's Minions Miniature Dachshunds

Photo Courtesy
of Aaron and Minette McGeehon

Their mellow, lovable nature tends to make Dachshunds a fairly easy addition to the family. Puppies are generally easy to introduce to new family members because they just want to love everyone. Adult Dachshunds can be a bit trickier, depending on their history; if they have been socialized, they generally won't be a problem. If not, introducing them into your home could be particularly interesting.

FUN FACT
Little Dog, Big Attitude

Dachshunds may do well in a family with other dogs, as long as they are smaller dogs. Note that Doxies may be possessive about toys and food, so introduce them to other pets with caution. Be certain to be generous with your affection among all your pets so your Dachshund does not become jealous and snappy.

In many cases, introducing your new Dachshund could be more about how your other dogs feel about another dog coming into the home. As long as your dogs love other dogs too, it will be incredibly easy to get them accustomed to each other. Make sure that your current dog's shots are up to date. It will be nearly impossible to keep them apart (your dog is going to be curious), so you will need to introduce them before bringing your new dog home. The best way to protect your puppy is to have your dog's shots current and a health check before the new pup arrives. Even if you adopt an adult, you should have your dog checked out to make sure everyone is healthy.

Even if all of the dogs involved tend to love other dogs, you are still going to need to follow the same process to introduce them. It is more a question of making sure that all of the dogs feel comfortable, including being on neutral ground during that first meeting. Have a plan for the first meeting to be on neutral ground, not at your home, no matter how friendly your current dog is. After that introduction, it will almost certainly be easy to start integrating your new dog into the fuzzy part of the family.

There are a number of benefits to already having a dog in your home. Even if you bring home an adult, your current dog can help teach your new Dachshund the rules. If you bring home a puppy, your current dog could be a great mentor to your puppy (depending on your dog's patience with puppies). Having another dog also makes socialization fairly easy because it's likely that your Dachshund will pick up on your other dog's listening to you, which could make it easier to get the Dachshund to listen. This works both ways though. If your current dog or dogs have any undesirable behaviors, you may want to try to work those out before your puppy arrives, too – you don't want your Dachshund learning bad habits.

Introducing Your New Puppy To Your Other Pets

Always introduce all new dogs to your current dog or dogs, regardless of age, in a neutral place away from your home. Even if you have never had problems with your current dog, you are about to change his world. Select a park or other public area where your dog will not feel territorial and plan to introduce your dog to the puppy there. This gives the animals the opportunity to meet and get to know each other before entering your home together.

When introducing your dog and puppy, make sure you have at least one other adult with you so there's a person to manage each canine. If you have more than one dog, then you should have one adult per dog. This will make it easier to keep all of the dogs under control. Even the best dogs can get overly excited about meeting a puppy. One of the people who needs to be there is the person who is in charge of the pets in your home (or people if you have more than one person in charge). This helps establish the pack hierarchy.

Don't hold your puppy when the dogs meet. While you may want to protect the puppy and make him feel comfortable by holding him, it has the opposite effect. Your puppy will likely feel trapped, with no way to escape. Being on the ground means that the puppy can run if he feels

Photo Courtesy of Deborah Perez

the need to. Stand near the puppy with your feet a little bit apart. That way, if the puppy decides he needs to escape he can quickly hide behind your legs.

Watch for raised hackles on your dog. The puppy and each dog should have a few minutes to sniff each other, making sure that there is always some slack in the leash. This helps dogs feel more relaxed since they won't feel like you are trying to restrain them. Your dog will probably either want to play or will simply ignore the puppy.

- If they want to play, just be careful that the dog doesn't accidentally hurt the puppy.

- If the dog ends up ignoring the puppy after an initial sniff, that is fine too.

If your dog's hackles are up or if he is clearly unhappy, keep the two apart until your dog seems more comfortable with the situation. Don't force the meeting.

The introduction could take a while, depending on each individual dog's personality. The friendlier and more accepting your dog is, the easier it will be to incorporate your new puppy into the home. For some dogs a week is enough time to start feeling comfortable together. For

Photo Courtesy of Kayley Von Der Lieth

other dogs, it could take a couple of months before they are fully accepting of a new puppy. Since this is a completely new dynamic in your household, your current dog may not be pleased with you bringing a little bundle of energy into his daily life. This is enough to make anyone unhappy, but especially a dog that has grown accustomed to a certain lifestyle. The older your dog is, the more likely it is that a puppy will be an unwelcome addition. Older dogs can get cranky around a puppy that doesn't understand the rules or doesn't seem to know when enough is enough. The goal is to make your puppy feel welcome and safe, while letting your older dog know that your love for him is just as strong as ever.

Once your new family member and the rest of the canine pack start to get acquainted and feel comfortable with each other, you can head home. As they enter the house, they will have a bit more familiarity with each other, making your current dogs feel more comfortable with the new addition to the family.

Once you are home, take the dogs into the yard and remove the leashes. You will need one adult per dog, including the puppy. If they seem to be all right or the dog is indifferent to the puppy, you can let your dog inside, re-leash the puppy, and keep the puppy on the leash as you go inside (after showing him where he is supposed to do his business).

Put the puppy in the puppy area when the introductions are done. Make sure your dogs cannot get into this area, and that your puppy cannot get out.

Introducing An Adult Dog To Other Animals

You always need to approach the introduction and first few weeks with caution. The new adult Dachshund will need his own stuff in the beginning, and should be kept in a separate area when you aren't around until you know that there won't be any fighting. If your dogs don't have much interest in being the boss and enjoy playing rough, it will take less time for your new Dachshund to fit into the pack.

Plan for the introduction to take at least an hour. It probably won't take that long, but you must make sure that all of the dogs are comfortable during the introduction. Since the dogs are all adults, they will need to move at their own pace.

Follow the same steps to introduce your current dogs with your new dog as you would with a puppy.

- Start on neutral territory.

- Have one adult human per dog present at the introduction (this is even more important when introducing an adult canine).

- Introduce one dog at a time – don't let several dogs meet your new Dachshund at the same time. Having multiple dogs approaching all at once in an unfamiliar environment with people the Dachshund doesn't know very well – you can probably see how this can be nerve-racking for any new dog.

Unlike with a puppy, make sure to bring treats to the meeting of two adult dogs. The animals will respond well to the treats, and you will have a way to quickly distract all of the dogs if they are too tense with each other.

During the introduction, watch the Dachshund and your dogs to see if any of them raises his hackles. This is one of the first really obvious signs that a dog is uncomfortable. If the Dachshund's hackles are up, back off the introductions for a little bit. Do this by calling your current dog back first. This is also when you should start waving treats around. Avoid pulling on the leashes to separate the dogs. You don't want to add physical tension to the situation because that could trigger a fight. Treats will work for all dogs present in the beginning, and your other dogs should be able to respond to your calling their names.

If any of the dogs are showing their teeth or growling, call your dog back and give the dogs a chance to settle down first. Use the treats and a calming voice to get them to relax. You want all the dogs to feel comfortable during the first meeting, so don't force the friendship. If they seem uncomfortable or wary at first, you will need to let them move at their own pace.

Older Dogs And Your Dachshund

If your current dog is older, keep in mind that puppies are energetic and likely to keep trying to engage the older dog in play. This can be very trying for your older canine. Make sure that your older dog isn't getting too tired of the puppy's antics because you don't want your puppy to learn to snap at other dogs. Watch for signs that your older dog is ready for some alone time, some time alone with you, or just a break from the puppy.

Once your Dachshund is ready to leave the puppy area for good, you will still want to make sure that your older dog has safe places to go to be alone in case he just doesn't feel up to being around a spry young thing. This will reduce the likelihood that your puppy will be repeatedly scolded and therefore learn to be wary of older dogs.

Even if you adopt an adult Dachshund, they can have a lot of energy and may want to play with other dogs around them. This can be a problem with older dogs, so make sure that your dog's golden years aren't marred by a new canine that has rules that don't make sense to your older dog and wants to play in a way your older dog can't.

Dog Aggression And Territorial Behaviors

Though they are known for being mellow, loving, and gregarious, Dachshunds can be surprisingly aggressive. Even more surprising, they appear on many lists of most aggressive dogs. Some Dachshund parents have reported aggression issues with their dogs at the age of six weeks old. It will be incredibly important that you learn how to properly train your Dachshund as soon as aggression presents itself. You cannot react with violence or harsh words because that reinforces aggression.

If not trained properly, dogs can take out their aggression on strangers. Some Dachshunds that are not properly socialized will be very suspicious around visitors. If you don't want to end up with a Dachshund that has to be put into isolation when you have company, you are going to have to learn how to train your dog. It isn't difficult to train a Dachshund to be that sweet

Photo Courtesy of Carolynn Hardcastle

little dog that people love; you just need to be prepared to be firm, consistent, and patient to help bring out your dog's friendly personality.

When people come to visit, you will need to tell them how to interact with your Dachshund. When a Dachshund feels threatened or afraid, he may lash out. Even if your Dachshund is perfectly trained, if someone picks up your dog, that can be a frightening experience for him. They look cute and cuddly, but that doesn't mean that they want to be han-

*Photo Courtesy
of Kristy L. Hamilton*

dled. Given how easy it is to injure a Dachshund's long back, you will need to be firm about how your visitors interact with your dog.

They may be small and friendly, but when afraid or hurt, Dachshunds will bark – or in worst cases bite. It takes a lot to end up on the most aggressive breeds list. The reason most people don't realize how aggressive they are is because they don't look very threatening. Given their history though, Dachshunds can be quite ferocious. Remember aggressive doesn't mean deadly, but it could still be dangerous. Other small breeds that are also considered aggressive include Jack Russell Terriers and Chihuahuas.

Do not use choke chains or other negative reinforcers on your Dachshund. Not only do those hurt your dog, but a Dachshund does not react well to negative reinforcement because he thinks for himself. What you teach your Dachshund with these types of restraints is that you don't know what you are doing and are using things to try to force your dog to behave in a certain way. What does work is treats and removal from any negative situation. Reward your dog for the good behavior, and the more often your dog does what you want him to do, the more often you reward him. Chapter 12 goes into how to train your Dachshund.

At home, you will need to be more careful. Despite his size, a Dachshund is not the kind of dog to back down, so if he feels that someone is challenging him or taking one of his toys, he may react aggressively. While he is young, it is easier to start to train against this kind of behavior, but an older dog will need extra monitoring and should not be left alone with other pets or children. An older Dachshund has to learn how to be a part of the pack and the proper way to react to people playing with toys and other items. This is why it is essential to always be firm and consistent.

There are two primary types of aggression that you should monitor for in your dog.

- Dominance aggression is when your dog wants to demonstrate control over another animal or person. This kind of aggression is shown through the following behaviors in reaction to anyone going near the Dachshund's belongings (like toys or a food bowl):

  - Growling

  - Nipping

  - Snapping

This is the behavior that the pack leader makes to warn others in the pack about touching his stuff. If your Dachshund reacts like this toward you, a family member, or another pet going close to his stuff, you must intervene immediately, correct him by saying "No," then lavish him with praise when he stops. You must consistently intervene whenever your Dachshund behaves in this manner.

Do not let the Dachshund be alone with other people, dogs, or animals as long as any of this type of behavior is exhibited. He will push boundaries, and if you aren't there to intervene, he will likely try to show his dominance in your absence.

You want to train your Dachshund not to react aggressively. Once you are sure the behavior has been eliminated, you can leave your dog and Dachshund alone for short periods of time, with you staying in another room or somewhere in close proximity, but out of sight. Over time, you can start to leave your pets alone when you go get the mail, then when you run errands. Eventually, you will be able to leave your Dachshund alone with other dogs without worrying that he or one of your other dogs will feel compelled to show dominance.

- Well socialized males are more interested in meeting and greeting other dogs. Unsocialized males can be aggressive and domineering. Females tend to be more predictable; they are more aloof even when properly socialized, but they are also less likely to be as aggressive or domineering when they are not socialized.

Your Dachshund will have to learn that the home is not just his. It belongs to people and the other dogs as well, and he is a part of the home, not the boss in your home.

Strong Natural Prey Drive

Having been bred to chase small animals down holes, it should not come as a surprise that Dachshunds can get very focused on other animals when they are outside. From squirrels and chipmunks to cats and other animals larger than them, Dachshunds may get a little overexcited and start to chase animals that make the mistake of running when they bark. While they can be fine with animals in your home, they may be more excitable when they are outside in the open air. Their long history could make walking a little trickier, even after they are properly socialized. While you won't have to worry too much about your dog pulling you over in an attempt to get a squirrel or other small animal nearby, you will need to prepare to train your dog to be less focused on those small animals. You don't want him to break the leash or slip his collar and get loose. They may not look it, but Dachshunds can run far faster than you might expect

You will also need to be careful about the introduction with cats, because of the chance that the cat will run. Dachshunds will almost certainly see that as a sign that it is playtime, so they will pursue the cat. It isn't so much about catching the cat as just having fun, but that doesn't mean that the cat will be pleased. Puppies will probably be easier to introduce to cats because their ability to run will be hampered by their short legs. You will need to plan to socialize your Dachshund puppy with the cat long before the puppy is allowed to run free in the home. Always be present when they interact so that you can correct the puppy's behavior.

It is unlikely that the prey drive will be a problem with your current pets, but you will want to be careful with your Dachshund and any rodents or smaller animals you have. Keep the cages for rodents too high for him to reach and away from anything that your dog could stand on. It isn't normal to have problems, but that doesn't mean it isn't possible. If you have other small animals, they will need to be kept in areas where your Dachshund cannot go. Rabbits, ferrets, and other pets typically are not trainable. Most small animals aren't able to learn not to run away, which your puppy will likely take as an invitation to play. Since smaller animals are usually in containers, this will make them less interesting to your Dachshund. It is when you are outside that you have to be more careful of your Dachshund's natural drive to chase. This means that you really should not allow your Dachshund off-leash without fencing. Even if you do have fencing, you will need to keep a close eye on your dog. If a small animal catches your Dachshund's attention, he may become focused on catching the creature.

Feeding Time Practices

Your Dachshund puppy will be fed in the puppy space, so mealtime will not be a problem in the beginning. When you start to feed the puppy with the other dogs, you can use the following suggestions to reduce the chance of territorial behavior with food.

STEPS TO ENSURE PEACEFUL EATING

1 SIMULTANEOUS BUT SEPARATE FEEDINGS

Feed your Dachshund at the same time as the other dogs, but in a different room. Keeping them separated will let your Dachshund eat without distractions or feeling that your other dogs will eat what is in his bowl. Make sure to feed your Dachshund in the same room each time, while the other dogs eat in their established room or rooms.

2 DON'T ALLOW FOOD SHARING

Keep your Dachshund and other dogs to their areas until they finish eating their food. Some dogs have a tendency to leave food in the bowl. Don't let them. They need to finish everything in the bowl because all food bowls will be removed as soon as the dogs are done eating.

3 STAY NEARBY, BUT DON'T DISTRACT

Make sure you have someone near your Dachshund so that he learns not to growl at people near the bowl. This will help to reduce stress when other dogs are around the food. If your dog demonstrates any aggression, immediately correct him by saying "No," then give him praise when he stops. Do not attempt to play with the food bowl, and make sure none of the kids play with it. Your dog needs to know that no one is going to try to steal his food.

4 SLOWLY MOVE THE DOGS CLOSER

Move the dogs closer together over a couple of weeks. For example, you can feed your current dog on one side of the door near the doorway and the Dachshund on the opposite side near the doorway.

5 FINALLY FEED IN THE SAME ROOM

After a month or two, you can feed the dogs in the same room, but with some distance between them. If your Dachshund starts to exhibit protective behavior with the other dogs, correct him, then praise him when he stops the behavior.

Eventually, you can start feeding the dogs close together. It can take weeks to months, depending on the age of the Dachshund when he comes to your home. A puppy will require less time because he will be socialized with the dogs from an early age, making him less wary. That does not mean that he won't display territorial behavior, but it likely won't take long for him to start to feel comfortable eating near the rest of the pack.

For adult dogs, it could take longer, and you should not rush it. Let your dog learn to feel comfortable eating before you make changes, even small ones. Dogs of any breed can be protective of their food, depending on what they have been through; this is exacerbated in protective breeds like the Dachshund. Your Dachshund needs to feel assured that this protective behavior is not necessary around other dogs before he will eat without incident. That means letting his confidence and comfort build at his own pace.

CHAPTER 8
The First Few Weeks

"After all puppy vaccines are complete, get them out and about. Meet people, meet other dogs. Puppy classes are a great way to start. At home, have people over many times so they get to know its ok to have others in your home."

Kim Gillet
Cameo Dachshunds

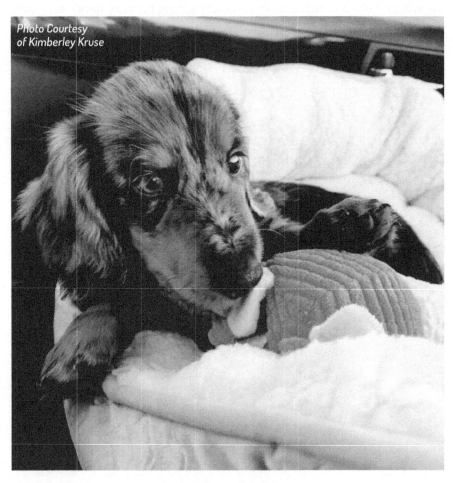

Photo Courtesy of Kimberley Kruse

S leeping is going to consume most of your Dachshund puppy's first week. The rest of the time will see your Dachshund puppy yo-yo-ing between excitement and nervousness. When your puppy begins to understand that your home is safe, his personality will start to show, and that is when things will get interesting. A Dachshund's intellect often shows as curiosity, and that means you are going to need to keep an eye on your pup.

At this time, you will also need to begin socialization (once the shots are completed) and training. If the breeder has already started house-training, you definitely want to keep using their method from the moment you get your pup home. It will already be a long struggle – make it a bit easier on yourself and your dog by keeping any existing momentum going.

The bond you start to build in the first week will continue to develop over the first month. By the end of the first month, your pup should be sleeping through the night and may have a fairly good understanding of where to go to the bathroom. You will also have a pretty good understanding of your canine's personality, which will make it a lot easier to know how to comfort the puppy during his infrequent bouts of uncertainty.

The first month is when you really need to start paying attention to your puppy's emerging personality. With a Dachshund, this will probably be when you start to notice that he will pick a favorite person. This doesn't mean your dog doesn't love the rest of the family, but he will be more comfortable with one person. Don't take it personally if you aren't the chosen favorite. It could mean that the favorite will need to take training very seriously and more responsibility may fall on that person's shoulders. That does not absolve the rest of the family of caring for the dog. Just because he has a favorite doesn't mean that he doesn't love the family, and he's probably going to want everyone to be together, especially when it comes to walking or play time.

Like with all intelligent breeds, when it comes to training, the key during this time is to remain consistent; that means everyone, not just the person who is the favorite. Use what you learn about your puppy's personality to encourage good behavior.

Photo Courtesy
of Roy Jordan

Setting The Rules And Sticking To Them

Your puppy needs to understand the rules and know that you and your family mean them. Dachshunds are often thinking and analyzing the situation. This means always taking a firm, consistent approach for both you and your dog. Once your canine learns to listen to you, training your Dachshund to do tricks will be a lot easier because he will want to have fun with his people. He will also be more likely to listen to you when he understands the home hierarchy. No matter how cute Dachshunds are when they look at you with those large eyes and floppy ears, for your sake and theirs, you need to let them know who is boss in a way that is firm, but not threatening.

HELPFUL TIP
Traveling

Some dog owners rely on medication for their dog while traveling. The American Veterinary Medical Association (AVMA) advises caution when using sedatives for your animal. Some sedatives may lead to respiratory or heart problems. Seek out advice from your veterinarian regarding safe approaches to traveling with your Dachshund.

Establish A No Jumping And No Mouthing Policy

If not properly trained, Dachshunds will bite children when they are afraid. It's your responsibility to ensure that your dog learns how to play properly, which means not jumping up on people or nipping them. Between their natural instincts and dental problems, it is also best to avoid playing tug-of-war. Any games that involve biting or nipping should always be avoided.

You also want to train your Dachshund not to jump because of the potential injury he could sustain to his back. This training begins from the very first week after their arrival.

Nipping
- One of the triggers for nipping is overstimulation, which can be one of the signs that your puppy is too tired to keep playing or training and you should put him to bed.

- Another trigger could be that your canine has too much energy. If this is the case, take your puppy outside to burn off some of his excess energy. At the same time, be careful not to over-exercise the puppy.

You need to be vigilant and immediately let your puppy know that nipping is not acceptable. Some people recommend using a water spritzer bottle and spraying the puppy while saying "No" after nipping. This is one of the few times when punishment may be effective, but you need to be careful that your dog doesn't associate it with anything other than the nipping.

Photo Courtesy of Karen Mayr

Always tell your puppy "No" firmly whenever he is nipping, even if it is during playtime. You should also pull away and say "Ouch!" loudly to let your puppy know that his teeth are hurting you. This will help to establish the idea that nipping is bad and is never rewarded.

Chewing

All puppies chew to relieve the pain of teething. Chewing can be an expensive problem for your dog to have, but it is fairly common with this breed. Whether he is chewing your furniture, utensils, or clothing, you want to discourage this behavior as quickly as possible.

- Make sure you have toys for your Dachshund (whether adult or puppy) so that you can teach him what things are acceptable to chew on. Having a lot of available toys, and rotating those toys out, will help give your puppy or dog a variety of options.

- If your puppy is teething, either refrigerate a couple of toys so they are cold, or give your puppy frozen carrots. The cold will help to numb the pain.

- Toys that are made either of hard rubber or hard nylon will be the best toys, particularly Kongs with kibble in them. You can even fill them with water and freeze them, which will give your puppy something cool to soothe the pain of teething.

For the most part, keeping your eye on your dog when he is not in his designated space will help you to quickly see when he is chewing on things he shouldn't. When this happens, say "No" firmly. If your dog continues to chew, put him back in his space. While he is in the space, make sure he has plenty of toys to chew on.

If you decide to use chew deterrents, such as different bitter and training sprays, be aware that some dogs will not care that an item tastes bad – they will chew anyway. Do not apply these deterrents and then leave your dog alone and expect him to just stop chewing. You need to see your dog's reaction before trusting that the bad habit is broken. Since Dachshunds are known for having separation anxiety, you will definitely want to find a way to alleviate the problem with chewing as quickly as possible so that your pup can be free to roam around your home. However, putting gross flavors on stuff isn't as much of a deterrent for them as you may expect. It is best to try to train them not to chew over spraying your possessions.

Jumping

Dogs typically jump on people when they first greet them. Use the following steps when you have a visitor (and if you can get someone who is willing to help, that will make the training that much easier).

STEPS TO ELIMINATING JUMPING UP ON VISITORS

1 **PUT A LEASH ON THE DOG**
when the person knocks on the door or rings the bell. The arrival of someone else will invariably excite most dogs, especially puppies.

2 **LET THE PERSON IN**
but do not approach the person with the puppy until he calms down.

3 **REINFORCE PROPER BEHAVIOR WITH PRAISE**
when the puppy keeps all four paws on the ground. Approach the visitor only after your Dachshund is calm.

4 **IGNORE INCORRECT BEHAVIOR**
Turn your body and ignore him when the puppy jumps up. Don't verbally correct him. Being completely ignored will be far more of a deterrent than any words you can say.

5 **USE DISTRACTIONS TO HELP THEM CALM DOWN**
Give your dog something to hold in his mouth if he does not settle down. Sometimes dogs just need a task to reduce their excitement. A stuffed animal or ball are ideal for distraction, even if your dog drops it.

6 **GET LOW AND PET YOUR DOG**
Having someone on his level will make him feel like he is being included. It also lets him sniff your face, which is part of a proper greeting. If your visitor is willing to help, this obvious acknowledgment can be a deterrent from jumping as the person is already on your dog's level.

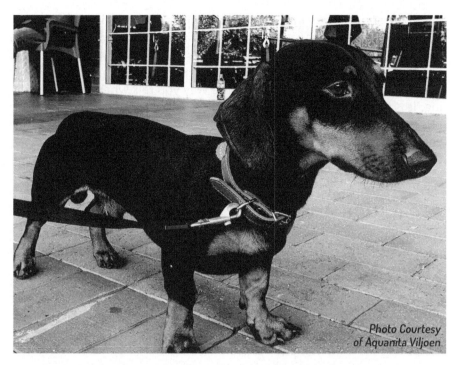

Photo Courtesy
of Aquanita Viljoen

Reward-Based Training Vs Discipline-Based Training

Other chapters detail the various aspects of training, but it is important to keep in mind just how much more efficient it is to train with rewards than with punishments, especially for an intelligent breed like the Dachshund. This will be a particular challenge as puppies can be exuberant and are easily distracted. It is important to remember that your puppy is young, so you need to keep your temper and learn when you need to take a break from training.

Several critical aspects that you will need to start working on during the first month:

- Housetraining (Chapter 9)

- Crate training (Chapter 6)

- Barking (Chapter 11)

Find out how much the breeder did in terms of housetraining and other such areas. The best breeders may even teach puppies one or two commands before they go home with you. If this is the case, keep using those same commands with your puppy so that the early training is not lost. This can help you establish the right tone of voice to use since the puppy will already know what the words mean and how to react to them. Once he understands that, he will more quickly pick up on other uses of that tone of voice as being the way you talk when you are training. It is another great way to let your little love know when you mean business versus when you want to play. These kinds of distinctions are easily picked up by a Dachshund and your dog will be more than happy to oblige.

Separation Anxiety In Dogs And Puppies

"Anxiety is sometimes common with Dachshunds. Dogs are pack animals and they want to be with the perceived pack. If you notice this in your new pup, start by trying to sit within eye-sight of the dog and then increase the distance over time. Then proceed to out of sight for short periods of time and return before they have time to get get anxious. Increasing the time with each session."

Mary Lee Wood
Zoey's Doxies

Dachshunds are not the kind of dog that does well when left alone. Between separation anxiety and their intelligence, they can do a lot of damage for such a small dog. You will want to plan to help your new dog know that everything will be just fine, even if you have to leave him alone for hours. Apart from making sure your dog is tired before you leave home, there are several ways you can prepare your puppy or dog for those longer days when he is left home alone.

In the beginning, keep the puppy's time alone to a minimum. The sounds of people moving around the house will help your Dachshund understand that the separation is not permanent. After the first week or so, alone time can involve you going out to get the mail, leaving the puppy inside by himself for just a few minutes. You can then lengthen the amount of time you are away from the puppy over a few days until the puppy is alone for 30 minutes or so at a time.

Here are some basic guidelines for when you first start to leave your puppy alone.

- Take the puppy out about 30 minutes before you leave.

- Tire the puppy out with exercise or playtime so that your leaving is not such a big deal.

- Place the puppy in the puppy area well ahead of when you go out to avoid having him associate the space with something bad happening.

- Don't give your puppy extra attention right before you leave because that reinforces the idea that you give attention before something bad happens.

- Avoid reprimanding your Dachshund for any behavior that happens while you are away. Reprimanding teaches him to be more stressed because it will seem like you come home angry.

If your Dachshund exhibits signs of separation anxiety, there are several things you can do to help make him comfortable during your absence.

- Chew toys can give your dog something acceptable to gnaw on while you are away.

- A blanket or shirt that smells like you or other family members can help provide comfort too. If you have worn the item and haven't gotten it very dirty, this is ideal, just make sure that you were not in contact with any chemicals over the course of the day you wore it. You also need to make sure that your dog won't eat the item in your absence. Consider giving him something that you know you won't wear again, in case he shreds it to pieces.

- Leave the area well lit, even if it is during the day. Should something happen and you get home later than you intended to, you don't want your little guy to be in the dark.

- Turn on a stereo (classical music is best) or television (old-timey shows that don't have loud noises, like Mr. Ed or I Love Lucy, work best) so that the house isn't completely quiet and unfamiliar noises are less obvious.

It will not take your Dachshund long to notice the kind of behaviors that indicate you are leaving. Grabbing your keys, purse, wallet, and other indications will quickly become triggers that can make your Dachshund anxious because he is going to quickly learn what these actions mean. Don't make a big deal out of it. If you act in a normal way, over time this will help your little one to understand that your leaving is fine and that everything will be all right.

*Photo Courtesy
of Gary and Jennifer Giller*

How Long Is Too Long To Be Left Home Alone?

You should not leave your dog home alone for more than eight hours at a time. He will likely be alright between four and eight hours, but any longer than that and he may start to have problems. This really isn't a breed you should get if you have to work long hours on a regular basis or if there won't be someone home more often than not.

One of the problems in the beginning is that your dog will need to be in a crate, and that means he will be crated for the entire time you are gone. Initially, this time should be very short. As your dog becomes housetrained and more trustworthy, your goal should be to allow your dog to be out of the crate so that it doesn't feel like a punishment. Your companion will not do well being trapped in a crate for hours at a time. You need to find some good mental games or things that your pup can do while you are gone to keep your Dachshund from being destructive. This is also why it is vital to ensure that you have your home properly prepared prior to your dog's arrival, especially if you get an adult Dachshund. Once your dog is crate trained and you start trying to leave him alone for longer periods of time, you want to make sure any destructive urges are put in check as much as possible.

Don't Overdo It, Physically Or Mentally

"Walking is always a good exercise for all Dachshunds. A puppy should start out slow and for only about 10 minutes because their muscles and bones are not fully developed. By six months old they could handle about a 30 minute walk. And by a year old they need about one hour of walking daily."

Mary Lee Wood
Zoey's Doxies

A tired puppy is a lot like a tired toddler; you have to keep the little guy from becoming exhausted or overworking those little legs. You need to be careful about harming your puppy's growing bones. Your pup is probably going to think that sleep is unnecessary, no matter how tired he is. It is up to you to read the signs that tell you when to stop all activities and put your pup to bed or take a break.

Photo Courtesy of Jessica Kyei-Yamoah

Training needs to be conducted in increments of time that your puppy or dog can handle. Be careful that you aren't pushing the training past the puppy's concentration threshold or that you aren't discouraging your adult dog with commands that are too advanced for him. If you continue training past your puppy's energy levels, the lessons learned are not going to be the ones you want to teach your dog. At this age, training sessions don't need to be long, they just need to be consistent.

Walks will be much shorter during that first month. When you go out, stay within a few blocks of home. Don't worry – by the month's end, your puppy will have a lot more stamina so you can enjoy longer walks and short trips away from home if needed. By the end of the first year you should be able to go for a short jog, depending on the advice from your vet. You can also do a bit of running on the leash in the yard if your puppy has a lot of extra energy. This will help your Dachshund learn how to behave on the leash while running. Puppies have a tendency to want to attack the leash because it is a distraction from running freely. They are good jogging companions, but when they get older taking them out for their own run can help to get rid of some of that energy and to keep them from getting overweight.

Some people do run with their Dachshunds, but that has to wait until your Dachshund is at least a year old. You can begin with those short little jogs once your pup has developed some stamina.

Just because your puppy can't take long walks initially doesn't mean that he won't have plenty of energy. Daily exercise will be essential, with the caveat that you need to make sure your puppy isn't doing too much, too soon. Staying active will help him to not only be healthy, but keep him mentally stimulated. You will quickly realize just how sedentary you have been if you have never had a dog before because you will be on the move almost all of the time the puppy is awake.

CHAPTER 9
Housetraining

While Dachshunds are known for being fantastic dogs to have as pets, they are notoriously difficult to housetrain. Whether you get a puppy or an adult, the housetraining is going to be at least as difficult as potty training a toddler, and you will need to be just as patient. They are an intelligent breed, and because of that some people say that Dachshunds train you, not the other way around. When it comes to housetraining your little companion, you have to let your Dachshund know that you are the one in charge and that your home is not a restroom.

Setting a schedule is going to be essential, and it needs to be one that you can keep so that your Dachshund knows when it will be alright to go to the bathroom. If you are consistent and firm (without being mean), it will really help your Dachshund understand what you are trying to teach him.

Using a leash can be helpful in ensuring that your puppy learns when and where to go, but there will still be challenges as you try to convince your puppy that there is a designated place to use the bathroom and it isn't in your home.

Make sure to consistently apply these two rules.

1. Never let the puppy roam the home alone – he should always be in the dedicated puppy space when you aren't watching him. Your Dachshund won't be pleased with the idea of being in a soiled crate, so that is a deterrent from doing his business when you are not around. He may not take the same approach to other areas of the home if he is left free to wander.

2. Give your puppy constant, easy access to the locations where you plan to housetrain him. You will need to make frequent trips outside as your puppy learns where to do his business, particularly if constant access to a place to use the restroom isn't possible. When you go out, put a leash on your puppy to make a point of where in the yard you want him to use the bathroom.

Always begin with a training plan, then be even stricter with yourself than you are with your puppy to keep that schedule. You are the key to the puppy learning where it is acceptable to do his business.

You Are In For A Challenge

Patience and consistancy are the keys. Keep an eye on your pup. You will notice the signs that they need to potty. Some of those signs are searching in a circle, starting to squat, and whining. Make sure to take them out after they wake, after they feed, and after they play."

Shona Malapelli
Malapelli's Minions Miniature Dachshunds

Even if you do everything right, some Dachshund parents report that they feel that they spend their Dachshund's life training him not to go to the bathroom in the home. Sometimes the problem is that a Dachshund has separation anxiety or some other problem. He isn't doing it to be malicious, he just doesn't know how to deal with being alone. Other times the problem is that the puppy parent failed to understand the dog's signals, so the puppy went inside because he couldn't continue to hold it.

Remember, your Dachshund is a small dog, so he doesn't have a large bladder. Dachshunds are intelligent, so setting up a consistent schedule will make it easier for your little guy to understand that going to the bathroom outside isn't meant to be an option, but mandatory. This will also help you to know when you need to get your little pup outside to avoid an accident.

There are many recommendations online, but, ultimately, the same, consistent process will work. This chapter focuses on the steps that are part of the foundation for succeeding.

> **Here's a quick list of the things that you are going to need to do, with more information provided a bit later in the chapter.**
>
> **1.** You should make sure that your Dachshund is crate trained (Chapter 6).
>
> **2.** Watch for signs that your puppy is looking for a spot to go to the bathroom.
>
> **3.** Set a schedule and always follow it. Your Dachshund will understand schedules and will start to expect the outings at the established times.
>
> **4.** Praise is both an effective tool and much healthier than treats, especially since the breed is prone to obesity. As soon as your pup responds to praise, start to move away from treats.
>
> **5.** Be patient. Every dog is different, so there is no way to predict how long housetraining will take. Being patient will help a lot more than getting frustrated or upset. Dachshunds react to human emotions, and housetraining will be that much more difficult if your dog starts to associate the training with negative emotions.

Inside Or Outside – Housetraining Options And Considerations

If your breeder has already started housetraining the puppy, stick to the method that the breeder used. This will increase the odds that housetraining will stick a little faster with your Dachshund.

You have the following housetraining options for your puppy:

- **Pee pads** – You should have several around the home for training, including in the puppy's area, but as far from his bed as possible.

- **Regular outings outside** – Organize these based on your puppy's sleeping and eating schedule.

- **Rewards** – You can use treats in the beginning, but quickly shift to praise.

In the beginning, the best way to housetrain your dog is to go out a lot of times, including at night, so that your puppy learns to keep all of his business outside. During the first few months, it is best to use a leash when you take the puppy out. This will help him learn to walk on a leash and keep him from getting distracted before he does his business.

A word of warning – don't start praising the puppy until he's done going to the bathroom. Interrupting him in mid-potty may make the puppy stop, increasing the odds that he will go again after you get back inside.

*Photo Courtesy
of Chloe Reynolds & Conor Chuck*

Setting A Schedule

You need to keep an eye on your puppy and consistently have house-training sessions:

- After eating

- After waking up from sleeping or each nap

- On a schedule (after it has been established)

*Photo Courtesy
of Wanita Raposo*

Photo Courtesy of Sandra Mazzafera

One of the most important things you can do is to watch your Dachshund for cues like sniffing and circling, two common activities as a puppy searches for a place to go. Start tailoring your schedule around your puppy's unique needs.

Puppies have small bladders and little control in the early days. If you have to initially train your pup to do his business inside, there needs to be a single designated space with a clean pee pad in the puppy's area, and you need to stock up on the appropriate pads for the puppy. Then make sure you change those pads regularly so your puppy does not get accustomed to having waste nearby. Pee pads are better than newspaper and can absorb more. Even if you use pads, you will still need to plan to transition to having the dog do his business outdoors as quickly as possible so that your Dachshund learns that indoors is the wrong place to go.

Choosing A Location

A designated restroom space can help make the experience of housetraining easier because your Dachshund will begin to associate one area of the yard for that one purpose, rather than sniffing around until he finds a choice spot. Having him go in one spot regularly will also make cleanup much simpler too; that way you can continue to use the whole yard instead of having to worry about stepping in waste.

Given how much Dachshunds love to dig, you should probably make the designated bathroom area away from the fences. Dachshunds can be very particular about weather, so having the designated area close to the door and under some kind of protection will greatly encourage your dog to always go outside – instead of going inside because he doesn't want to be out in the inclement weather.

When you are out for walks is the perfect time to train your puppy to go to the bathroom. Between walks and the yard, your puppy will come to see the leash as a sign that it is time to relieve his bladder, which could become a Pavlovian response.

Make sure that you pay attention to your puppy the entire time you are outside. You need to make sure that he understands the purpose of going outside is to go to the bathroom. Do not send your puppy outside alone and assume that he's done what you wanted him to do. Until there are no more accidents in the home, you need to verify that your puppy isn't losing focus while he is outside.

Keyword Training

All training should include keywords, even housetraining. You and all members of the family should know what words to use when training your dog where to go to the bathroom, and you should all be using those words consistently. If you have paired an adult with a child, the adult should be the one using the keyword during training.

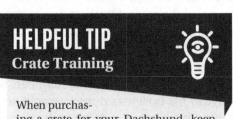

HELPFUL TIP
Crate Training

When purchasing a crate for your Dachshund, keep in mind the length of your dog. A longer crate will be necessary for your Doxie to get up and turn around comfortably. Keeping your dog crated when he is alone, while you're at work, or when you are sleeping, is helpful with house-training. Dachshunds are difficult to train, so be persistent in using the crate effectively.

To avoid confusing your puppy, be careful not to select words that you often use inside the home. Use a phrase like "Get busy" to let your puppy know it's time to get to work, not something that involves the word "bathroom" or "potty"– these are words that you will likely say in casual conversation, which could trigger your dog to go when you don't mean for him to go. "Get busy" is not a phrase most people use in their daily routine, so it is not something you are likely to say when you don't mean for your puppy to use the bathroom.

Once your puppy learns to use the bathroom based on the command, make sure he finishes before offering praise or rewards.

Reward Good Behavior With Positive Reinforcement

Positive reinforcement is very effective. In the beginning, take a few pieces of kibble with you when you are teaching your puppy where to go, both inside and outside the home. Learning that you are the one in charge will help teach your Dachshund to look to you for cues and instructions.

Part of being consistent with training means lavishing the little guy with praise whenever your puppy does the right thing. If you gently lead your puppy to the area on a leash without any other stops, it will gradually become obvious that your Dachshund should go there to use the bathroom. Once you get outside, encourage your pup to go when you get to the place in the yard that is intended to be his bathroom spot. As soon as he does his business, give him immediate and very enthusiastic praise. Pet your puppy as you talk to let the little guy know just how good the action was. Once the praise is done, return inside immediately. This is not playtime. You want your puppy to associate certain outings with designated potty time.

While praise is far more effective for Dachshunds, you can also give your puppy a treat after a few successful trips outside. Definitely do not make treats a habit after each trip because you do not want your Dachshund to expect one every time he does his business. The lesson is to go outside, and the puppy can learn that such outings may include treats.

The best way to housetrain in the first month or two is to go out every hour or two, even at night. You will need to set an alarm to wake you within that time to take the puppy outside. Use the leash to keep the focus on using the bathroom, give the same enthusiastic praise, then immediately return inside and go to bed. It is difficult, but your Dachshund will get the hang of it a lot faster if there isn't a long period between potty breaks. Over time, the pup will need to go outside less frequently, giving you more rest.

If your Dachshund has an accident, it is important to refrain from punishing the puppy. Accidents are not a reason to punish – it really reflects more on your training and schedule than on what the puppy has learned. That said, accidents are pretty much an inevitability. When it happens, tell your puppy, "No. Potty outside!" and clean up the mess immediately. Once that is done take the puppy outside to go potty. Of course, if your puppy doesn't go, he doesn't get any praise.

Cleaning Up

Clean up any messes in the home as soon as you find them. Unless you catch your puppy using the bathroom in the home, there is no point in negative reinforcement. Your dog will simply learn to hide his mess to avoid being punished. Take the dog outside instead and see if he will

Photo Courtesy
of Alma Diaz

use the bathroom. If someone is home, it is best to clean up the mess as quickly as possible. Spend a bit of time researching what kinds of cleaner you want to use, whether generic or holistic. For example, you will likely want to get a product with an enzyme cleaner. Enzymes help to remove stains by speeding up the chemical reaction of the cleaner with the stain. It also helps to remove the smell faster, reducing the odds that your dog will continue to go to the bathroom in the same place. Dachshunds don't have an issue with marking their territory, especially if they are properly trained, but you may want to discourage dogs that are visiting from claiming areas where your puppy has had accidents. Enzyme cleaners are best for cleaning up puppy accidents.

Pay attention to when these accidents happen and determine if there is a commonality between them. Perhaps you need to add an additional trip outside for your puppy or should make a change in his walking schedule. Or maybe there is something that is startling your dog, causing an accident.

CHAPTER 10
Socialization

"They need to be socialized early in life. A good breeder will start this process 3 weeks by introducing them to different sights, smells, and sounds. They need this socialization time from 3 to 18 weeks. Take them places that will be a positive experience for them. Start slow and increase the time with each visit."

Mary Lee Wood
Zoey's Doxies

Although, as discussed in an earlier chapter, Dachshunds can be aggressive, most are enthusiastic about meeting and enjoying the company of others. The best way to bring out the fun-loving, playful pup in your Dachshund is to start socializing your dog as soon it is safe to do so (puppies will need all of their shots before you expose them to dogs outside of your home on a regular basis). This is a breed that loves company and tends to be optimistic and playful. Regular socialization will bring out the best in your dog so that you have the loving playful dog you want.

Photo Courtesy
of Jeanne Brigandi
Photo by Carl Brigandi

Photo Courtesy of Frances Brown

When done early, socialization for Dachshunds is incredibly easy because they are such an affable, gregarious breed. Dachshunds' fun-loving temperament will make it easy, but you still want to approach socialization with caution to ensure that it is a positive experience for everyone.

Like any dog, Dachshunds can be bossy, possessive, and jealous, though they aren't known for it. Sometimes the terrier or bulldog does come out, and then the experience can be a little less than enjoyable. If you start early, you can nip this in the bud, making it fun for both you and your pup. It could be a bit more of a challenge if you get an adult that hasn't been properly socialized.

Socialization allows your Dachshund puppy to learn that it can be a lot of fun to play with people you invite into your home and dogs that you encounter out on your walks. To make sure the best in your Dachshund's personality comes out, you have to plan to start socialization from a very early age.

Remember that your puppy will need to have all of his vaccinations before being exposed to other dogs.

Socialization Can Make Life Easier In The Long Run

All dogs need socialization, but intelligent breeds have more analytical minds, so you want them to learn as early as possible that most of the time the world is a safe place and that other people and animals usually don't pose a threat. It will also help for your puppy to learn that acting in a dominant, aggressive way is not acceptable.

The benefit of early socialization is that it can make life that much more enjoyable for everyone involved, no matter what the situation is. A socialized dog will approach the world from a much better place than a dog that is not socialized.

Photo Courtesy of Karen Mayr

Greeting New People

Training your Dachshund on how to treat visitors may take a little longer because he may not be in the mood for any social interaction – and people are going to want to pet your adorable little dog. It will be just as important to let people know how to interact with your dog as it is to train your dog how to interact with visitors. Let your visitors know to leave the dog alone if the dog is not showing any interest in an introduction.

HELPFUL TIP
Socializing

Dachshunds are instinctively suspicious of strangers. They need extensive exposure to new people, places, and other animals. Continue exposure to new sights through adolescence (six to nine months), and offer socialization from ages one to three when emotional and physical changes may cause aggression.

Puppies will likely enjoy meeting new people, so make sure to invite people over to help socialize your canine family member. To introduce your puppy to a new person, try one of these methods:

1. Try to have your puppy meet new people daily, if possible. This could be during walks or while you are doing other activities when you get out of the house. If you can't meet new people daily, try for at least 4 times a week.

2. Invite friends and family over, and let them spend a few minutes just giving the puppy attention. If your puppy has a favorite game or activity, let people know so that they can play with him. This will win the little guy over very quickly and teach him that new people are fun and safe to be with.

3. Once your puppy is old enough to learn tricks (after the first month – don't try to teach him tricks immediately; he needs a bit more time and you will need to see if his personality is a good fit for tricks), have your little friend demonstrate the tricks for visitors. This will be really important even though your puppy won't get much bigger because a lot of people are nervous around dogs of any size.

4. Avoid crowds for the first few months. When your puppy is several months to a year old, attend some dog-friendly events so that your pup can learn not to be uncomfortable around a large group of people.

Greeting New Dogs

"I have found many Dachshunds do not like big dogs unless raised with them. They tend to be very aggressive with them and can get themselves into trouble."

Kim Gillet
Cameo Dachshunds

Photo Courtesy
of Vicki Sanchez

Chapter 7 covers the introduction of your new Dachshund with your other dogs, but meeting dogs who aren't part of your home is a little different, especially since you can encounter them when you are out walking. Most dogs will bow and sniff each other during an introduction. Watch for the same signs of aggression covered in Chapter 7, such as raised hackles and bared teeth. Bowing, high tail, and perked ears usually mean that your Dachshund is excited about meeting the dog. If your Dachshund is making noises, watch for the signs of aggression to make sure that the sounds are of play, not unease.

According to the Dachshund Society, about a third of Dachshunds have been reported to be aggressive toward other dogs (none of them were aggressive to people). If your Dachshund is aggressive, you want to train him early so that this isn't an issue. The best way to do that is with playdates at a neutral place. This will remove any jealousy about sharing toys or territorial tendencies.

Don't let your Dachshund jump up on other dogs. If he does, immediately say "No," to let him know that is not acceptable behavior. This can become a way of showing dominance, which you really don't want with your pup, even if it is just play in the beginning.

The Importance Of Continuing Socialization

Even friendly dogs need to be socialized. Making sure the puppy gets exposure to other people and other dogs is important to keep him from getting too aggressive or dominant. This doesn't mean forcing him into interaction, but joining classes and setting up playdates will give your dog a reason to be excited about meeting other dogs.

Have family and friends visit regularly, especially bringing their dogs along, so that your Dachshund has constant reminders that his home is a welcoming place, not somewhere that he needs to exert his dominance. You don't want your pup to feel that the outside world is fine, but that he can be a little terror at home.

Socializing An Adult Dog

Sometimes an adult dog will be too set in his ways to change, particularly if your dog is in his golden years. However, most adult dogs can be socialized as long as you make it your top priority (along with training). If you aren't prepared to be very patient with your Dachshund adult, then it is best not to adopt an adult. There is a chance that your Dachshund won't be as friendly with other dogs, even if he seems to be alright with other dogs at the rescue facility. Before you can begin to socialize your dog, you need to make sure he already knows some basic commands and that you have him under control before any introductions are made.

Socializing an adult canine requires a lot of time, dedication, gentle training, and a firm approach. You may be lucky enough to get an adult that is already well socialized. However, that does not mean that you can be entirely relaxed. The dog may have had a bad experience with a particular breed of dog that no one knows about.

***

If you have problems with your adult dog, consult a behaviorist or specialized trainer. For instance if you have to avoid dogs during that first week because your Dachshund is not reacting well to them, a professional will help you learn how to better socialize your adult dog.

5
TIPS FOR CONTINUED SOCIALIZATION

TIP 1 — **MASTER THE BASIC COMMANDS**

Your dog should be adept at the following commands before you work on socialization: *Sit, Down, Heel, Stay.* Stay is especially important because if your dog can remain in one place based on your commands, then he is demonstrating self-control, something that will be very helpful for socialization because you can override an aggressive impulse by activating the listening mode. When you go outside, you will need to be very aware of your surroundings, and be able to command your dog before another dog or person gets near.

TIP 2 — **USE A SHORT LEASH ON WALKS**

At the first sign of aggression, turn and walk in the opposite direction. Being aware of your surroundings will start to cue you into what your dog is reacting to so you can start training your dog not to react negatively.

TIP 3 — **CHANGE DIRECTION**

if you notice that your Dachshund is not reacting well to a particular person or dog approaching you. Avoidance is a good short term solution until you know that your dog is more accepting of the presence of these other dogs or people.

If you aren't able to take a different direction, tell your dog to sit, then block your dog's view. This can prove to be very challenging as your dog will try to look around you. Engage in training to get your dog to listen to you, taking his mind off of what is coming toward him.

TIP 4 — **SCHEDULE PLAY DATES WITH FRIENDLY DOGS**

Ask friends with friendly dogs to visit you, then meet in an enclosed space. Having one or two friendly dogs interact with your dog can help your Dachshund to see that not all dogs are dangerous or need to be put in their place. Having the dogs walk around the area together without a lot of interaction can help your dog learn that other dogs are usually just interested in enjoying the outside, so there is no reason to try to bully them.

TIP 5 — **GET SPECIAL TREATS JUST FOR WALKS**

If your dog is aggressive when walking, have him sit, and give him one of the special treats. Dachshund are food motivated, so this could be a perfect way of distracting your dog from whatever is making him feel protective. At the first snarl or sign of aggression, engage the training mentality and draw upon your dog's desire for those special treats. This method is slow, but it is reliable over time because your dog is learning that the appearance of strangers and other dogs means special treats, a positive experience, not a negative one. However, this does not train the dog to interact with those dogs. You can couple it with the fourth suggestion to get the best results.

CHAPTER 11
Training Your Dachshund

"Every dog is different but, in general, Dachshunds can be stubborn. Be consistent with every accept of training. Most are food driven and will do anything for a treat. Be patient and they will become a well trained dog."

Mary Lee Wood
Zoey's Doxies

The breed's intelligence coupled with a love for food and play means that your Dachshund can be bribed to do just about anything. He will love the attention, but there may be times when your dog just doesn't feel like listening, no matter what bribe you offer. This is one reason to always be careful about how many treats you give your Dachshund (the other reason being the risk of getting overweight or obese).

Dachshunds can be fantastic to train for many types of skills. They love playing, they love being around you, though they may feel that training is more about training you – they want treats or toys, so they are willing to do what you ask in order to "make you" give them the treats or toys. Their natural enthusiasm for doing new things and spending time with their people is all they need to make them happy. Their stubbornness can occasionally make it a bit more of a challenge, but keep your cool.

HELPFUL TIP
Training the Owner

There are many ways to train dogs. If you are a new pet owner, you may benefit from the advice of a professional trainer. Never train your dog by instilling fear because you may only build anxiety in your pet. For the sake of balance, do not overdo love and affection either. Provide a balanced, structured routine.

While training will get increasingly more enjoyable over time, it will likely be slow going in the beginning as your dog will be quite excited for the interaction. You will need to be firm and consistent, as well as keeping the training sessions very short in the beginning. If you are patient with your pup from the start, you will find that it will pay off later.

Photo Courtesy of Jessica Kyei-Yamoah

Benefits Of Proper Training

In addition to making socialization and general excursions easier, training could be a way of saving your dog's life. Understanding commands will help to stop your dog from running into the street or from responding to provocations from other dogs (or from acting as the aggressor). Training could also be a time saver in the event your dog gets away from you.

Training is a great way to bond with your dog. It gives you dedicated time together and helps you to understand your puppy's developing personality and to learn what kinds of rewards will work best for other tasks, like socialization. This is a dog that can join you when you go out for picnics or on other outings, so you want to make sure your Dachshund is trained so that you can enjoy a full range of activities.

Choosing The Right Reward

"Don't expect them to learn like a German Shepherd would. Instead, they require lots of praise, lots of treats, and lots of reasons why you want them to do this or that. Otherwise you will be ignored."

Kim Gillet
Cameo Dachshunds

The right reward for a Dachshund will ultimately be love and affection. Treats are the easiest way of keying a puppy into the idea that performing tricks is a good behavior. Soon, though, you will need to switch to something that is a secondary reinforcer. Praise, additional playtime, and extra petting are all fantastic rewards for Dachshunds. Your dog will probably follow you around until you decide to just sit back and relax. Plopping down to watch a movie and letting your puppy sit with you is a great reward after an intense training session. Not only did your puppy learn, but you both now get to relax together.

Photo Courtesy of Brittany Prince

Remember, this is a breed that is prone to obesity, which can be detrimental to both your dog's health and back. Make sure that you switch to a different kind of positive reward as early as possible. Dachshunds love their toys too, so you don't have to solely rely on praise (something that may or may not be a good reward depending on your dog's mood or preferences).

If you would like your Dachshund to attach positive feedback with a sound, you can use a clicker. They are relatively inexpensive and need to be used at the same time as you praise your puppy or dog. Clickers are not necessary, but some trainers find them useful.

Photo Courtesy
of Bob Jenkins Jr.

Name Recognition

Over time, many of us come up with multiple names for our dogs. Nicknames, joke names, and descriptions based on some of their ridiculous actions (it's why we love them) can all be used later. However, before you can train a dog, you have to make sure your dog understands his real name.

1. Get some treats and show one to your dog.

2. Say the dog's name, immediately say "Yes" (your dog should be looking at you when you speak), then give your dog a treat.

3. Wait 10 seconds, then show your dog a treat and repeat step 2.

Sessions shouldn't last longer than about five minutes because your dog will lose either focus or interest. Name recognition is something you can do several times over the day. After you have done this over five to ten sessions, the training will change a bit.

1. Wait until your dog isn't paying attention to you.

2. Call your dog. If the dog has a leash on, give it a gentle tug to get your dog's attention.

3. Say "Yes" and give the dog a treat when he looks at you.

During this time, do not speak your dog's name during corrections or for no real reason. This is because in the beginning, you need to get the dog to associate the name only with something very positive, like treats. This will more quickly program your dog to listen to you no matter what else is going on around him.

It is likely that your Dachshund will not require a lot of time before he recognizes his name.

Essential Commands

There are five basic commands that all dogs should know. These commands are the basis for a happy and enjoyable relationship with your dog. By the time your puppy learns all five of the commands, the correlation between the words you say and the expected actions will be more obvious. This will clue the dog in to understanding new words in terms of expectation and will make it much easier to train him on the more complex concepts.

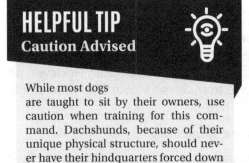

HELPFUL TIP
Caution Advised

While most dogs are taught to sit by their owners, use caution when training for this command. Dachshunds, because of their unique physical structure, should never have their hindquarters forced down into a sitting position. Keep training fun, and you will be rewarded with an obedient and happy Doxie.

Train your puppy to do the commands in the order they appear in this chapter. Sit is a basic command, and something all dogs already naturally do. Since dogs sit often, it is the easiest command to teach. Teaching leave it and drop it is much more difficult, and it usually requires that the puppy fight an instinct or desire. Consider how much you give in to something you want to do when you know you shouldn't – that's pretty much what you are facing, but with a puppy. Quiet can be another difficult command as dogs (particularly puppies) tend to bark as a natural reaction to something. These two commands will take longer to teach, so you want to have the necessary tools already in place to increase your odds of success.

Here are some basic guidelines to follow during training.

- Include everyone in the home in the Dachshund training. The puppy must learn to listen to everyone in the household, and not just one or two people. A set training schedule may only involve a couple of people in the beginning, especially if you have children. There should always be an adult present for training, but including one child during training will help reinforce the idea that the puppy must listen to everyone in the house. It is also a good way for a parent to monitor a child's interaction with the puppy so that everyone plays in a way that is safe and follows the rules.

- To get started, select an area where you and your puppy have no other distractions, including noise. Leave your phone and other devices out of range so that you keep your attention on the puppy.

- Stay happy and excited about the training. Your puppy will pick up on your enthusiasm, and will focus better because of it.

- Be consistent and firm as you teach.

- Bring a special treat to the first few training sessions, such as pieces of chicken or small treats.

Sit

Start to teach sit when your puppy is around eight weeks old. Once you settle into your quiet training location:

1.   Hold out a treat.

2. Move the treat over your puppy's head. This will make the puppy move back.

3.   Say "sit" as the puppy's haunches touch the floor.

Having a second person around to demonstrate this with your puppy will be helpful as they can sit to show what you mean.

Wait until your puppy starts to sit down and say sit as he sits. If your puppy finishes sitting down, give praise. Naturally, this will make your puppy incredibly excited and wiggly, so it may take a bit of time before he will want to sit again. When the time comes and the puppy starts to sit again, repeat the process.

It's going to take more than a couple of sessions for the puppy to fully connect your words with the actions. Commands are something completely new to your little companion. Once your puppy has demonstrated mastery over sit, start teaching down.

Down

Repeat the same process to teach this command as you did for sit.

1.   Tell your dog to sit.

2.   Hold out the treat.

3.   Lower the treat to the floor with your dog sniffing at it. Allow your pup to lick the treat, but if he stands up, start over.

4. Say down as the puppy's elbows touch the floor, then give praise while letting your puppy eat the treat.

Wait until the puppy starts to lie down, then say down. If the Dachshund finishes the action, offer your chosen reward.

It will probably take a little less time to teach this command.

Wait until your puppy has mastered down before moving on to stay.

Stay

Stay is a vital command to teach because it can keep your puppy from running across a street or from running at someone who is nervous or scared of dogs. It is important that your dog has mastered sit and down before you teach stay. Learning this command is going to be more difficult since it isn't something that your puppy does naturally. Be prepared for it to take a bit longer.

1. Tell your puppy to either sit or stay.

2. As you do this, place your hand in front of the puppy's face.

3. Wait until the puppy stops trying to lick your hand before you begin again.

4. When the puppy settles down, take a step away. If your puppy is not moving, say stay and give a treat and some praise.

Giving your puppy the reward indicates that the command is over, but you also need to indicate that the command is complete. The puppy has to learn to stay until you say it is okay to leave the spot. Once you give the okay to move, do not give treats. Come should not be used as the okay word as it is a command used for something else.

Repeat these steps, taking more steps further from the puppy after a successful command.

Once your puppy understands stay when you move away, start training to stay even if you are not moving. Extend the amount of time required for the puppy to stay in one spot so that he understands that stay ends with the okay command.

When you feel that your puppy has stay mastered, start to train the puppy to come.

Come

This is a command you can't teach until the puppy has learned the previous commands. Before you start the training session, decide if you want to use come or come here for the command. Be consistent in the words you use.

This command is important for the same reason as the previous one. If you are around people who are nervous around dogs, or encounter a wild animal or other distraction, this command can snap your puppy's attention back to you.

1.   Leash the puppy.

2.   Tell the puppy to stay.

3.   Move away from the puppy.

4.   Say the command you will use for come and give a gentle tug on the leash toward you.

Repeat these steps, building a larger distance between you and the puppy. Once the puppy seems to understand it, remove the leash and start at a close distance. If your puppy doesn't seem to understand the command, give some visual clues about what you want. For example, you can pat your leg or snap your fingers. As soon as your puppy comes running over to you, offer a reward.

Off

Although Dachshunds are small, it's important to train your dog to get down or off something. This is not the same as teaching your dog not to jump on people (Chapter 8). This command is specifically to get your dog off furniture or surfaces that may be too dangerous. This is training that you will need to be prepared to do on the fly because you are training your dog to stop an action. This means you have to react to that undesirable action. Having treats on hand will be essential when you see your dog getting up on things you don't want him to be on.

1.   Wait for your dog to put his paws on something that you don't want him on.

2. Say "Off" and lure him away with a treat that you keep just out of his reach.

3. Say "Yes" and give him a treat as soon as his paws are off the surface.

Repeat this every time you see the behavior. It will likely take at least half a dozen times before your dog understands he should not perform the action anymore. Over time, switch from treats to praise or playing with a toy.

Leave It

This is a difficult training command, but you need to teach your dog leave it for when you are out on a walk and want him to ignore other people or dogs.

1. Let your dog see that you have treats in your hand, then close it. Your fist should be close enough for your dog to sniff the treat.

2. Say "Leave it" when your dog starts to sniff your hand.

3. Say "Yes" and give your dog a treat when he turns his head away from the treats. Initially, this will probably take a while as your dog will want those treats. Don't continue to say "Leave it" as your dog should not be learning that you will give a command more than once. You want him to learn that he must do what you say the first time you say it, which is why treats are recommended in the beginning. If a minute or more passes after giving the command, you can then issue it again, but make sure your canine is focused on you and not distracted.

These sessions should only last about five minutes and it will take your dog some time to learn, as you are teaching him to ignore something he does naturally. When he starts to understand and looks away when you say leave it without spending much time sniffing, you can move on to more advanced versions of the training.

1. Leave your hand open so that your dog can see the treats.

2. Say "Leave it" when your dog starts to show interest (this will probably be almost immediately, especially since you won't have your hand closed, so be prepared).

   a. Close your fist if your dog continues to sniff or gets near the treats in your hand.

   b. Give your dog a treat from your other hand if he stops.

Repeat these steps until your dog finally stops trying to sniff the treats. When your dog seems to have this down, move on to the most difficult version of this command.

1. Place treats on the ground, or let your dog see you hide them, and stay close to those treats.

2. Say "Leave it" when your dog starts to show interest in sniffing the treats.

   a. Place a hand over the treats if he doesn't listen.

   b. Give him a treat from your hand if your dog does listen.

From here, you can start training while standing further from the treat with your dog leashed so you can stop him if needed. Then start to use other things that your dog loves, such as a favorite toy or another tempting treat that you don't usually give him.

Drop It

This is going to be one of the most difficult commands you will teach your puppy because it goes against both your puppy's instincts and interests. Your puppy wants to keep whatever he has, so you are going to have to offer him something better instead. It is essential to teach the command early though, as your Dachshund could be very destructive in the early days. Furthermore, this command could save your pooch's life. He is likely to lunge at things that look like food when you are out for a walk and this command will get him to drop anything potentially hazardous that he picks up.

Start with a toy and a treat, or a large treat that your dog cannot eat in a matter of seconds, such as a rawhide. Make sure the treat you have is one that your puppy does not get very often so that there is motivation to drop the toy or big treat.

1. Give your puppy the toy or large treat. If you want to use a clicker too, pair it with the exciting treat that you will use to help convince your puppy to drop the treat.

2. Show your puppy the exciting treat.

3. Say "Drop it" and when he drops the treat or toy, tell him good and hand over the exciting treat while picking up the dropped treat or toy.

4. Repeat this immediately after your puppy finishes eating the exciting treat.

You will need to keep reinforcing this command for months after it is learned because it is not a natural instinct. You should also start using food that your dog finds almost irresistible. This is one of those rare times when you must use a treat because your puppy needs something to convince him to drop a cherished toy, or, more importantly, food that he shouldn't be eating.

Quiet

You want to ensure your pup doesn't become a nuisance, especially if you are in an apartment. Initially, you can use treats sparingly to reinforce quiet if your pup enjoys making noise.

1. When your puppy barks for no obvious reason, tell him to be quiet and place a treat nearby. It is almost guaranteed that the dog will fall silent to sniff the treat.

2. If your dog does fall silent, say "Good dog" or "good quiet."

It will not take too long for your puppy to understand that quiet means no barking.

If you want your Dachshund to be more of a watchdog, you will need to provide some guidance on when he should bark. For example, you can teach him to bark when people come to the door (you will need to get a friend or another family member to help you so that he doesn't bark when family arrives). You should have a professional help you with this one as it is a more advanced type of training, and Dachshunds all react differently. A professional can help tailor the approach to training your dog when to bark at people at the door. Otherwise, you will want your dog to know that he shouldn't be randomly barking at birds at the window or squirrels running around in the yard.

Where To Go From Here

Dachshunds are a breed that is fairly easy to train, so you may not need to take your dog to any classes. As often as not, they will be able to pick up on what you want to train without any other help. However, they will enjoy the extra socialization if you want to take them to a puppy or obedience class. It is a safe environment and a great opportunity for both of you to learn, and there will be an expert present to instruct you in the best way to teach your pup how to act.

Puppy Classes

Puppies can begin to go to puppy school as early as 6 weeks. This is the beginning of obedience training, but you will need to be careful about interactions with other dogs until your puppy has completed his vaccinations. Talk with your vet about when is a good time to begin classes, or at least a safe time. Your vet may be able to recommend good puppy training classes in your area.

The primary purpose of these classes is socialization. Studies have shown that a third of puppies have minimal exposure to new people and dogs during the first 20 weeks of their life, which can make the outside world scarier. The puppy classes give you and your puppy a chance to learn how to meet and greet other people and dogs in a strictly controlled environment. Dogs that attend these classes are much friendlier and are less stressed about things like large trucks, loud noises, and visitors. They are also less likely to be nervous or suffer from separation anxiety.

It is also good training for you. In the same studies, people who attended these classes were better able to react appropriately when a puppy was disobedient or misbehaved. The classes teach you how to train your puppy and how to deal with the emerging headstrong nature of your dog.

Many classes will help you with some of the basic commands, like sit and down. Look for a class that also focuses on socialization so that your puppy can get the most out of the class.

Obedience Training

After your puppy graduates from puppy school and understands most of the basic commands, you can switch to obedience classes. Obedience classes are more difficult, but it shouldn't be that much of a challenge for a Dachshund. Some trainers offer at-home obedience training, but it is best to find a class so that your dog can continue socialization as a part of his training. If your puppy attends puppy classes, the trainers can provide you with the next classes that they recommend. Dogs of nearly any age can attend obedience training classes, though your dog should be old enough to listen.

Obedience training usually includes the following:

- Teaching or reinforcing basic commands, like sit, stay, come, and down.

- How to walk without pulling on the leash.

- How to properly greet people and dogs, including not jumping on them.

Obedience school is as much about training you as training your dog. It helps you learn how to train while getting your dog through basic commands and how to behave for basic tasks, like greetings and walking. Classes usually last between 7 and 10 weeks.

Ask your vet for recommendations. If your vet doesn't have any recommendations, take time to thoroughly research your options. Look at the following details when evaluating trainers:

- Are they certified, particularly the CPDT-KA certification?

- How many years have they been training dogs?

- Do they have experience with training Dachshunds?

- Can you participate in the training? If the answer is no, do not use that trainer. You have to be a part of your dog's training because the trainer is not going to be around most of your dog's life. Therefore, your dog has to learn to listen to you.

Obedience training does not help with serious behavioral issues. If your dog has anxiety, depression, or other serious behavioral issues, you need to hire a trainer to help your dog work through those issues. Do your research to make sure your selected trainer is an expert, preferably with experience with intelligent, strong-willed dogs. If possible, find someone who has experience dealing with Dachshunds.

Once your Dachshund has the basic commands down and has done well in obedience training, you can start to do other more enjoyable training. As long as your Dachshund did well in the classes, you should not need a trainer because your dog will listen to you. With a foundation for commands and a more active interest in learning more, this could be a great foundation for doing more – as long as your Dachshund is interested. By this point, you should be able to tell if your dog is interested, and you will definitely have more of an idea if you want to pursue more difficult training given your dog's personality.

CHAPTER 12
Nutrition

Dachshunds love food, but their stomachs tend to be fairly unforgiving. Those sensitive stomachs are just one reason why you have to be very careful about what and how much your Dachshund eats. For the sake of your dog's health (and your nose), you need to take their dietary needs very seriously. High-quality diets will help to keep your dog healthy and happier.

Since the breed is prone to obesity, you will need to keep a close eye on what your Dachshund eats. It is far too easy to give too many treats, especially if everyone in your family "trains" the dog. If everyone becomes accustomed to training the dog with praise or toys instead of treats, then your dog's weight and stomach will be far less problematic. Since your dog is always near you, it will be easy to think that throwing him the occasional fry is fine. As you will soon learn, his stomach probably won't agree. Plus, you don't want to teach a smart dog that food on your plate is fair game because that simply increases the risk that your dog will learn to take food when you leave food unattended.

Photo Courtesy
of Sandra Mazzafera

Why A Healthy Diet Is Important

Most Dachshunds can be convinced to do virtually anything within their abilities with the promise of food. This is where their love of food and small stature really start to undermine their health. All of the caution you take so that you don't injure your dog's back can be undermined by your pup getting too heavy for his small frame.

You need to be aware of roughly how many calories your dog eats a day, including treats. Get accustomed to regularly weighing your dog so that you are aware of his weight – that way you know when he is putting on the pounds. You can also establish regular weight checks at home because Dachshunds fit on home scales, though you may need to be a little creative (without picking up your pup) if your Dachshund is longer than your scale. This will key you in to when you should adjust how much food your Dachshund eats a day, or change his food to something with more nutritional value, but fewer calories.

Dangerous Foods

Dogs can eat raw meat without having to worry about the kinds of problems a person will encounter. However, there are some human foods that could be fatal to your Dachshund. You should keep these foods away from all dogs:

- Apple seeds
- Chocolate
- Coffee
- Cooked bones (they can kill a dog when the bones splinter in the dog's mouth or stomach)
- Corn on the cob (the cob is deadly to dogs; corn off the cob is fine)
- Grapes/raisins
- Macadamia nuts
- Onions and chives
- Peaches, persimmons, and plums
- Tobacco (your Dachshund will not know that it is not a food and may eat it if it's left out)
- Xylitol (a sugar substitute in candies and baked goods)
- Yeast

In addition to these potentially deadly foods, there is a long list of things that your dog shouldn't eat. The Canine Journal has a lengthy list of foods (http://www.caninejournal.com/foods-not-to-feed-dog/) that should be avoided.

Canine Nutrition

The dietary needs of a dog are significantly different from a human's needs. People are more omnivorous than dogs, meaning they require a wider range of nutrients to be healthy. Canines are largely carnivorous, and protein is a significant dietary requirement. However, they need more than just protein to be healthy.

The following table provides the primary nutritional requirements for dogs.

Nutrient	Sources	Puppy	Adult
Protein	Meat, eggs, soybeans, corn, wheat, peanut butter	22.0% of diet	18.0% of diet
Fats	Fish oil, flaxseed oil, canola oil, pork fat, poultry fat, safflower oil, sunflower oil, soybean oil	8.0 to 15.0% of diet	5.0 to 15.0% of diet
Calcium	Dairy, animal organ tissue, meats, legumes (typically beans)	1.0% of diet	0.6% of diet
Phosphorus	Meat and pet supplements	0.8% of diet	0.5% of diet
Sodium	Meat, eggs	0.3% of diet	0.06% of diet

The following are the remaining nutrients dogs require, all of them less than 1% of a puppy's or adult's diet:

- Arginine
- Histidine
- Isoleucine
- Leucine
- Lysine
- Methionine + cystine
- Phenylalanine + tyrosine
- Threonine
- Tryptophan
- Valine
- Chloride

It is best to avoid giving your dog human foods with a lot of sodium and preservatives.

Water is also absolutely essential to keeping your dog healthy. There should always be water in your dog's water bowl, so make a habit of checking it several times a day so that your dog does not get dehydrated.

Proteins And Amino Acids

Since dogs are carnivores, protein is one of the most important nutrients in a healthy dog's diet (although they should not eat meat nearly as exclusively as their close wolf relatives; their diets and needs have changed significantly since they became companions to humans).

Proteins contain the necessary amino acids for your dog to produce glucose, which is essential for giving your dog energy.

A lack of protein in your dog's diet will result in him being lethargic. His coat may start to look dull and he is likely to lose weight. Conversely, if your dog gets too much protein, your dog's body will store the excess protein as fat, meaning he will gain weight.

Meat is typically the best source of protein, and it is recommended since a dog's dietary needs are significantly different from a human's needs. However, it is possible for a dog to have a vegetarian diet as long as you ensure that your dog gets the necessary protein through other sources, and you will need to include supplemental vitamin D in his food. If you plan to feed your dog a vegetarian diet, talk to your vet first. It is incredibly difficult to ensure that a carnivore gets adequate protein with a vegetarian diet, especially puppies, so you will need to dedicate a lot of time to research and discussion with nutrition experts to ensure that your dog is getting the necessary proteins for his needs.

Fat And Fatty Acids

Photo Courtesy
of Mavourneen Smith

Most of the fats that your dog needs also come from meat, though seed oils can provide a lot of the necessary healthy fats too, with peanut butter being one of the most common sources. Fats are broken down into fatty acids, which your dog needs for fat-soluble vitamins that help with regular cell functions. Perhaps the most obvious benefit of fats and fatty acids is in your dog's coat, which will look and feel much healthier when your dog is getting the right nutrients.

There are a number of potential health issues if your dog does not get adequate fats in his daily diet.

- His coat will look less healthy.

- His skin may be dry and itchy.

- His immune system could be compromised, making it easier for your dog to get sick.

- He may have an increased risk of heart disease.

The primary concern if your dog gets too much fat is that he will gain weight and become obese, leading to additional health problems. For breeds that are predisposed to heart problems, you need to be particularly careful to ensure your dog gets the right amount of fats in his diet. An estimated 18% of Dachshunds have heart problems.

Carbohydrates And Cooked Foods

Dogs have been living with humans for millennia, so their dietary needs have evolved like our own. They are able to eat foods with carbohydrates to supplement the energy typically provided by proteins and fats. If you cook up grains (such as barley, corn, rice, and wheat) prior to feeding them to your dog, it will be easier for your dog to digest those complex carbohydrates. This is something to keep in mind when considering what type of food you will feed your dog as you want to get a kibble (dry dog food) that uses meat instead of grains; while your dog can digest food with grains, he won't get as much of the nutritional value as he would from food that contains real meat.

Different Dietary Requirements For Different Life Stages

"Be careful not to over feed your Dachshund. Most will need to switch from puppy food to adult food around 8 months the of age or they will be likely to gain too much weight. Keep them slim, but filled out. You should be able to feel their ribs but not see them."

Shona Malapelli
Malapelli's Minions Miniature Dachshunds

Different stages of a dog's life have different nutritional needs:

- Puppies
- Adults
- Senior dogs

Puppy Food

Dog food manufacturers produce a completely different type of food for puppies for a very good reason – their nutritional needs are much different than their adult counterparts. During roughly the first 12 months of their lives, puppies' bodies are growing. To be healthy, they need more calories and have different nutritional needs to promote that growth.

HELPFUL TIP
Weight Issues

Dachshunds are prone to becoming overweight. Miniature Doxies should weigh about 11 lbs. at one year of age. Standard Dachshunds' weight should fall between 16-32 lbs. at one year old. It is important to provide protein-rich food for your dog while avoiding carbohydrates and high-fiber foods. Measuring your dog's food, providing smaller portions, and exercising daily will help ensure your Doxie is in the correct weight range.

Adult Dog Food

The primary difference between puppy food and adult dog food is that puppy food is higher in calories and nutrients that promote growth. Dog food manufacturers reduce these nutrients in food made for adult dogs as they no longer need to sustain growth. As a general rule, when a dog reaches about 90% of his predicted adult size, you should switch to adult dog food.

The size of your dog is key in determining how much to feed him. The following table is a general recommendation on how much to feed your adult Dachshund a day. Initially, you may want to focus on the calories as you try to find the right balance for your dog.

Dog Size	Calories
10 lbs.	420 during hot months 630 during cold months
20 lbs.	700 during hot months 1,050 during cold months
30 lbs.	900 during hot months 1,400 during cold months

Notice that no Dachshund needs more than 900 calories in the hot months, and they all need less than 1,500 even when it is cold. This is not a lot of food, so you need to be very aware of how many calories you are giving your dog to ensure he maintains a healthy weight. This scale is for a dog's ideal weight range. If your dog is overweight or obese, ask your vet about how much you should be feeding your dog per day.

Also keep in mind that these recommendations are per day, and not per meal. Whether you feed your dog once a day or several times per day, make sure that you carefully measure out how much food you give so that you do not exceed the daily recommendation.

If you plan to add wet food, pay attention to the total calorie intake and adjust how much you feed your dog between the kibble and wet food. In other words, the total calories in the kibble and wet food should balance out so as not to exceed your dog's needs. The same is true if you give your dog a lot of treats over the course of the day. You should factor treat calorie counts into how much you feed your dog at mealtimes.

If you plan to feed your dog homemade food, you will need to learn more about nutrition, and you will need to pay close attention to calories, and not cup measurements.

Senior Dog Food

Senior dogs aren't always capable of being as active as they were in their younger days. If you notice your dog slowing down or see that your dog isn't able to take longer walks because of joint pain or a lack of stami-

Photo Courtesy
of Thomas Gaudet & Makenzie Carty

na, that is a good sign that your dog is entering his senior years. Consult with your vet when you think it is time to change the type of food you give your dog.

The primary difference between adult and senior dog food is that senior dog food has less fat and more antioxidants to help fight weight gain. Senior dogs also need more protein, which will probably make your dog happy because that usually means more meat and meat flavors. Protein helps to maintain your dog's aging muscles. He should be eating less phosphorous during his golden years to avoid the risk of developing hyperphosphatemia. This is a condition where dogs have excessive amounts of phosphorous in their bloodstream, and older dogs are at greater risk of developing it. Phosphorous is largely found in bones to help with muscle contractions and the nerves. The level of phosphorous in the body is controlled by the kidneys. As such, elevated levels of phosphorous are usually an indication of a problem with the kidneys.

Senior dog food has the right number of calories for the reduced activity, so you shouldn't need to adjust how much food you give your dog, unless you notice that he is putting on weight. Consult your vet before you adjust the amount of food or if you notice that your dog is putting on weight. This could be a sign of a senior dog ailment.

Your Dog's Meal Options

You have three primary choices for what to feed your dog, or you can use a combination of the three, depending on your situation and your dog's specific needs:

- Commercial food
- Raw diet
- Homemade diet

Commercial Food

Make sure that you are buying the best dog food that you can afford. Take the time to research each of your options, particularly the nutritional value of the food, and make this an annual task. You want to make sure that the food you are giving your dog is quality food. Always account for your dog's size, energy levels, and age. Your puppy may not need puppy food as long as other breeds and dog food for seniors may not be the best option for your own senior Dachshund.

Pawster provides several great articles about which commercial dog foods are good for Dachshunds. Since new foods frequently come on the market, check back occasionally to see if there are newer, better foods available. Since you have to be careful of your Dachshund's weight, it is well worth verifying that you are giving him the best food available.

If you aren't sure about which brand of food is best, talk with the breeder about what foods they recommend. Breeders are really the best guides for you here, as they are experts on the breed, but you can ask your vet as odds are they have worked with Dachshunds.

Some dogs may be picky, and they can certainly get tired of having the same food repeatedly. Just as you switch up your meals, you can change what your Dachshund eats. While you shouldn't frequently change the brand of food, you can get foods that have different flavors. You can also change the taste by adding a bit of wet (canned) food. This is an easy change to make, giving your dog a different canned food (usually just about 1/4 to 1/3 of the can for a meal, depending on your dog's size) with each meal.

For more details on commercial options, check out Dog Food Advisor. They provide reviews on the different brands, as well as providing information on recalls and contamination issues.

Commercial Dry Food

Dry dog food often comes in bags, and it is what the vast majority of people feed their dogs.

Dry Dog Food

PROS	CONS
• Convenience	• Requires research to ensure you don't buy doggie junk food
• Variety	
• Availability	• Packaging is not always honest
• Affordability	• Recalls for food contamination
• Manufacturers follow nutritional recommendations (not all of them follow this, so do your brand research before you buy)	• Loose FDA nutritional regulations
	• Low quality food may have questionable ingredients
• Specially formulated for different canine life stages	
• Can be used for training	
• Easy to store	

The convenience and ease on your budget means that you are almost certainly going to buy kibble for your dog. This is perfectly fine, and most dogs will be more than happy to eat kibble. Just know what brand you are currently feeding your dog, and pay attention to kibble recalls to ensure you stop feeding your dog a particular food if necessary. Check out the following sites regularly to make sure your dog's food has not been recalled:

- Dog Food Recalls – Dog Food Advisor

- American Kennel Club

- Dog Food Guide

Commercial Wet Food

Most dogs prefer wet dog food to kibble, but it is also more expensive. Wet dog food can be purchased in larger packs that can be very easy to store.

Like dry dog food, wet dog food is convenient, and picky dogs are much more likely to eat it than kibble. When your dog gets sick, it is best to use wet dog food to ensure that he is eating so that he gets the nec-

Wet Dog Food

PROS	CONS
• Helps keep dogs hydrated	• Dog bowls must be washed after every meal
• Has a richer scent and flavor	
• Easier to eat for dogs with dental problems (particularly those missing teeth) or if a dog has been ill	• Can soften bowel movements
	• Can be messier than kibble
	• Once opened, it has a very short shelf life, and should be covered and refrigerated
• Convenient and easy to serve	
• Unopened, it can last between 1 and 3 years	• More expensive than dry dog food, and comes in small quantities
• Balanced based on current pet nutrition recommendations	
	• Packaging is not always honest
	• Recalls for food contamination
	• Loose FDA regulations

essary nutrition each day. It may be a bit harder to switch back to kibble once he is healthy, but you can always continue to add a little wet food to make each meal more appetizing to your dog.

Raw Diet

For dogs like Dachshunds that have food allergies, raw diets can help to keep your dog from having an allergic reaction to wheat and processed foods. Raw diets are heavy in raw meats, bones, vegetables, and specific supplements. Some of the benefits to a raw diet include:

- Improves your dog's coat and skin

- Improves immune system

- Improves health (as a result of better digestion)

- Increases energy

- Increases muscle mass

Raw diets are meant to give your dog the kind of food he ate before being domesticated. It means giving your dog uncooked meats, whole (uncooked) bones, and a bit of dairy products. It doesn't include any processed food of any kind – not even food cooked in your kitchen.

There are potential risks to this diet. Dogs have been domesticated for millennia, and their digestive system has evolved as they have. Trying to force them back on the kind of diet they used to eat does not always work as intended because they may not be able to fully digest it anymore. There are also a lot of risks with feeding dogs uncooked meals, particularly if the food has been contaminated. Things like bacteria pose a serious risk and can be transferred to you if your dog gets sick. Many medical professionals also warn about the dangers of giving dogs bones, even if they are uncooked. Bones can splinter in your dog's mouth, puncturing the esophagus or stomach.

The Canine Journal provides a lot of information about the raw diet, including how to transition your current dog to this diet and different recipes for your dog.

Homemade Diet

If you regularly make your own food (from scratch, not with a microwave or boxed meal), it really doesn't take that much more time to provide an equally healthy meal for your companion.

Keeping in mind the foods that your Dachshund absolutely should not eat, you can mix some of the food you make for yourself into your Dachshund's meal. Just make sure to add a bit more of what your Dachshund needs into the food bowl. Although you and your Dachshund have distinctly different dietary needs, you can tailor your foods to include nutrients that your dog needs.

Do not feed your Dachshund from your plate. Split the food, placing your dog's meal into a bowl so that your canine understands that your food is just for you. The best home-cooked meals should be planned in advance so that your Dachshund is getting the right nutritional balance.

Typically, 50% of your dog's food should be animal protein (fish, poultry, and organ meats). About 25% should be full of complex carbohydrates. The remaining 25% should be from fruits and vegetables, particularly foods like pumpkin, apples, bananas, and green beans. These foods provide additional flavor that your Dachshund will probably love while making him feel full faster, so that the chance of overeating is reduced.

The following are a few sites you can use to learn to make meals for canines. Some of them are not Dachshund specific, so if you have more than one dog, these meals can be made for all of your furry canine friends:

- Cuteness.com: How to Make Dog Food for a Dachshund

- Recipe: Homemade Dog Food for Dachshunds

- Life with Dogs
- DORG Daily Diet
- Dogsaholic

Scheduling Meals

Your Dachshund will likely expect you to stick to a schedule, and that definitely includes mealtimes. This is a breed that will have no problem with letting you know you are late with the food. If treats and snacks are something you establish as normal early on, your dog will believe that treats are also a part of the routine and will expect them.

Food Allergies And Intolerance

Whenever you start your dog on a new type of dog food (even if it is the same brand that your dog is accustomed to, but a different flavor), you need to monitor him as he becomes accustomed to it. Food allergies are fairly common, so you will need to be aware of the symptoms. Food allergies in dogs tend to manifest themselves as hot spots, which are similar to rashes in humans. Your dog may start scratching or chewing specific spots on his body. His fur could start falling out around those spots.

Some dogs don't have a single hot spot, but the allergy shows up on their entire coat. If your Dachshund seems to be shedding more fur than normal, take your dog to the vet to have him checked for food allergies.

If you do give your dog something that his stomach cannot handle, it will probably be obvious when your dog is unable to hold his bowels. If he is already housetrained, he will probably either pant at you or whimper to let you know that he needs to go outside. Don't ignore either of these pleas. Get him outside as quickly as you can so that he does not have an accident. Flatulence will probably occur more often if your Dachshund has a food intolerance.

Since the symptoms of food allergies and tolerances can be similar to a dog's reaction to nutritional deficiencies (particularly a lack of fats in a dog's diet), you should visit your vet if you notice any problems with your dog's coat or skin.

CHAPTER 13
Loving And Loyal, Your Pup Will Love To Play

"Dachshunds gain weight easy so daily exercise is a must."

Kim Gillet
Cameo Dachshunds

Dachshunds are incredibly loyal and loving dogs, which is a large part of why they are so popular (as well as that adorable appearance). Their high energy levels mean it is essential for you to have plenty of games to play. Fortunately, their size means that they aren't going to need hours of exercise every day.

They may not be quite as clownish as pugs and Boston Terriers, but they are more intelligent, which means you can get them involved in more complicated games. Some Dachshunds love to do tricks, and others prefer games. Bribery is one way to get them to do things like tricks – food works alarmingly well, and you will need to use it sparingly. Fortunately, praise can be fairly effective too. Dachshunds really just love to be with their people, and giving them a chance to use their brains is almost always welcome.

Most of the time, people are told to train certain behaviors out of their dogs, but you don't have to do that in every case. Dachshunds have a lot of potentially undesirable behaviors, such as chasing and digging. Instead of training them not to do these things, you can use their instincts to entertain them and yourself.

This chapter covers the many different games and activities you and your Dachshund can enjoy to best play to their strengths and natural abilities.

Photo Courtesy
of Gabrielle Lemos

Exercise Needs

Bringing a Dachshund into your home means you are agreeing to daily exercise, even when he is still a puppy. Dogs don't want to misbehave, but if they are bored, mischief is inevitable. Fortunately, their size makes exercising enough pretty easy, so when you finally leave your dog home alone, it's unlikely that your furniture or other things will be shredded in your absence.

Since weight problems are directly related to a lack of exercise, if your dog is gaining weight, that could be a sign that he isn't getting enough time moving about. Fortunately, it's easy to correct that. You have a lot of options for how to make sure your dog gets enough of a workout – it is much easier (and healthier) to do more with your dog than to just measure calories.

Photo Courtesy
of Sami Bain

Photo Courtesy of Erin Green

A Wide, Easy Activity Range

Their appearance and inquisitive personality makes Dachshunds a popular breed. They love to explore new areas. Still, the more different activities that you do with your dog, the happier you will both be. Just remember to carry water with you and don't let your dog get too hot.

Outdoor Games

Though you do need to be careful of their backs, Dachshunds are fairly sturdy dogs that love running and playing outside. Your little guy will love to be out romping in nice weather. Things like Frisbee and fetch are the kinds of games that will tire your pup while using very little of your own energy. You will need to get discs and balls that are easy on your dog's teeth.

Agility Training

Better known as obstacle courses, agility training is a great way to keep your adult dog running and happy. You get to guide your dog through the course, helping not only to build your bond, but also to give your dog a chance to feel more comfortable when he is outside the

Photo Courtesy of Meg Giger

home. Since you are the one in control, and your dog will likely be confused in the beginning, be prepared to look a bit silly at first. The point is to have fun and to keep your dog engaged, so getting and keeping his attention is key to being successful.

Two to three hours of dedicated time are recommended a week, with one of those hours going to a weekly class. The more you can train at home, the better your dog will do in this sport.

Chase

Considering Dachshunds were bred to chase and capture, this is a perfect game for your little athletic tube dog. Get rid of that extra energy while teaching your dog what is alright to chase. This one will take a bit of set-up, but it will be worth it.

Get a nylon rope and attach it to the toy you plan to use for the game. You can also look for a toy that already has a rope to avoid the preparation part. Drag the toy behind you, kind of like getting a cat's attention. It won't take long before your pup understands what it is you are trying to do and starts to chase you and the toy.

When your Dachshund catches the toy, stop and praise the little guy for a job well done. You don't want this to devolve into a tug of war, so you should stop when your Dachshund catches the toy. Eventually your dog will get good enough that you will be able to swing the toy around you while you sit down (being very careful so that you don't hit your dog or anyone else) and let your Dachshund do all of the moving. He won't get tired of just running in circles until you stop.

If you play inside, make sure that there is nothing that your dog can run into so that he doesn't run into something and get hurt.

Digging

Convincing Dachshunds not to dig is like trying to get a retriever not to chase a ball – it is virtually impossible to convince them not to do it. Instead of trying to fight something your dog is probably going to do if given a couple of seconds alone in the yard, you can create a space just for him to follow his digging instincts. You can add sand or mulch to an area away from fences or the borders of your home and let your dog do what he loves to do.

To encourage your dog to play just in that spot, you can bury toys, then watch him find them. This will be both mentally stimulating and physically tiring, so you can end the game with a nice belly rub session and a bit of peace and quiet.

If it is a rainy or cold day, you can always set up a little pillow fort inside and hide the toy in that. Your dog will have an absolute blast, and you will likely have a great time heartily laughing at the enthusiastic display in finding that toy.

Fetch

Dachshunds get very enthusiastic about chasing down something you throw because of the very excited response you have when they return with it. The interaction is fun and chasing after the ball is perfect for tiring out your dog. Dachshunds are also inclined to chase and return stuff to you because they are hunters by nature.

You may want to keep fetch to an outdoor activity, especially if you have kids, so that objects around your home don't get broken. If so, you can never slip up and allow fetch on a rainy day because that will teach your Dachshund that you can be convinced to give in with the right tactics.

Photo Courtesy of Angela Gaines

Playtime! And More Playtime!

"Dachshunds don't need a lot of exercise to be happy, but they do need it to keep their weight down. Playing fetch and going for walks are great ways to keep them entertained and fit."

Elizabeth Bender
BenderDachs

Just because there is inclement weather doesn't mean that your dog's energy levels will be any lower, or that boredom won't set in, so you'll need to plan to keep your dog's exercise schedule consistent, even when you are stuck inside the house. Of course, if you can put your dog out to play in the snow in a backyard, that will be fantastic as he can tire himself out in his excitement. During rain and heat, you need to find the right activities to tire your canine without going outside for extended periods of time. Here are some alternatives to help expend your Dachshund's energy.

1. If you don't want to use a toy for chase, you might be able to get your Dachshund to chase a laser pointer. This may or may not work as your Dachshund may realize that he can't catch it. If he doesn't seem to mind though, it is a great way to get rid of that energy on rainy or cold days.

2. Hide and seek is a game you can play once your dog knows about proper behavior in the home, whether you have him find you or a favorite toy you've hidden.

3. Puzzle toys are a great way to get your dog to move around without you having to do much. Many games come with treats, and knowing Dachshunds, it won't be long before your dog figures out how to get the food out of the toy, so make sure you rotate various puzzles at playtime. Use these kinds of toys sparingly to avoid piling on the extra calories.

4. Treat hunting is something that you can do easily inside and that will be very exciting for your dog. With Dachshunds, you can play a game that focuses on hunting and gathering since that is what they were bred to do – hunt game and make sure it got back home. Your dog will have time for something to help get rid of the energy while engaging that clever little brain. Just show your pup that you have a treat, then let him watch you hide it. Of course, he will find it quickly and you should lavish him with praise for this. After a couple of times, have someone distract your pup as you hide the treat you just showed him. This helps your Dachshund to learn the point of the game, and it will probably become a favorite. Since you have to be careful with food, you can exchange the treat for something like an old sock or shoe – something that will have a strong scent but that you won't mind getting a bit chewed up during the game. You can even teach your Dachshund what the object is by always saying the name when you hold it up to sniff.

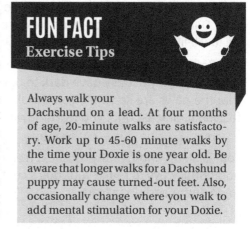

FUN FACT
Exercise Tips

Always walk your Dachshund on a lead. At four months of age, 20-minute walks are satisfactory. Work up to 45-60 minute walks by the time your Doxie is one year old. Be aware that longer walks for a Dachshund puppy may cause turned-out feet. Also, occasionally change where you walk to add mental stimulation for your Doxie.

CHAPTER 14
Grooming – Productive Bonding

"Both Longhair and Smooth-Coated Dachshunds do shed. Wirehair Dachshunds, like other wired coats, do not. Maintenance of a Smooth-Hair Dachshund is easy, with regular baths and brushing to remove the short stiff hairs before they shed. Using a 'slicker' brush on a Longhair will remover the undercoat and dandruff and decrease shedding dramatically. Bathing and using a light conditioner will keep their coat glossy."

Elizabeth Bender
BenderDachs

When it comes to grooming, it really doesn't get much easier than the Dachshund, depending on the type of coat your Dachshund has. You won't need to hire a professional groomer for your Dachshund's coat, unless you have a long-haired dog and you want his hair styled. The classic short-haired Dachshund is one of the easiest coats to groom in the dog world. Wire-haired coats are somewhere in the middle, but they are still easy to manage.

Do be aware that Dachshunds don't tend to enjoy being groomed. If you can convince your puppy to enjoy it, you won't have to fight with your Dachshund as much when he becomes an adult. When he gets older, it will likely be a lot easier since he will enjoy the extra attention.

Getting your Dachshund's nails clipped will likely be another issue. Given that they usually have dark to black fur on their paws, and the fact that the paws are so small, you should start by taking your pup to a professional, at least until you learn how to clip his nails.

This chapter provides a baseline for making sure your Dachshund's coat is clean and healthy, but feel free to look online and elsewhere for additional ways to make your dog's coat really shine if you have the time to do some additional care.

Grooming Tools

You don't need too many tools to properly groom your Dachshund. Make sure you have the following items on hand before your puppy or adult dog arrives:

- You will need to tailor the type of brush to the type of coat your Dachshund has:
  - For short-haired Dachshunds, a soft bristled brush is best.
  - For long-haired Dachshunds, a slicker brush works well, then follow it up with a bristled brush after you finish the first brushing. It is a longer endeavor to take care of your long-haired dog's coat since the coat tends to get matted, particularly around the ears.
  - For wire-haired Dachshunds, a short napped wire bristle brush is best.
  - For any type of coat, you can also get a rubber palm brush or mitt to make the experience more like petting. If you have a wire-haired breed, you will want to make sure to use the recommended brush during the spring and fall when the longer-haired breeds tend to shed more.

- Shampoo (check Pawster and Breedsy for the latest recommendations for a breed with potential skin conditions) – use mild shampoo specifically for dogs.

- Nail trimmers

- Toothbrush and toothpaste (check the American Kennel Club for the latest recommendations) – use toothpaste made specifically for dogs.

Coat Management

While Dachshunds do shed, they are considered moderate shedders. There is some variation based on their coat type, but given their size, you aren't going to have the vast amounts of fur everywhere as you would with some larger dogs.

If you have allergies, Dachshunds do shed enough to potentially trigger those allergies.

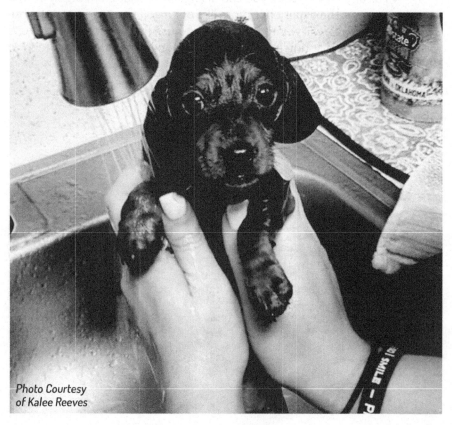

Photo Courtesy of Kalee Reeves

Photo Courtesy
of Tamara Hanson

Puppies

Regardless of the type of fur your Dachshund has, grooming a puppy is fairly universal, and their coats are fairly easy to manage – even if it is a little difficult to get them to stop squirming. Daily brushing can not only reduce how much your puppy sheds, but it helps you to build a bond with the dog. Yes, it will be a bit challenging in the beginning because puppies don't sit still for long periods of time. There will be a lot of wiggling and attempts to play. Trying to tell your puppy that the brush is not a toy clearly isn't going to work, so be prepared to be patient during each brushing session.

HELPFUL TIP
Grooming Needs

Dachshunds are available in smooth, long, and wirehaired coats. Smooth-coated Dachshunds require little grooming other than a weekly brushing. Wirehaired and long-coated dogs will need more bathing and professional grooming. Don't forget your Doxie's ears! They are prone to infection and need regular attention.

On the other hand, your pup will be so adorable, you probably won't mind that grooming takes a bit longer. Just make sure you let your pup know that this is a serious effort and playing comes after grooming. Otherwise, your Dachshund is going to always try to play, which will make brushing him more time consuming. Plan to brush your puppy after a vigorous exercise session so that your Dachshund has far less energy.

Adult Dogs

You will have a different grooming regimen based on your Dachshund's coat. If you have a long-haired Dachshund, grooming is a daily occurrence, whereas the other two coat types require brushing less frequently.

Regardless of the type of Dachshund you have, make sure that you do not bathe him too often. One of the reasons that Dachshunds don't tend to get as dirty as you might expect (given how low to the ground they are) is because they produce a special fat that protects them. This was necessary given the kinds of elements they were accustomed to when they were used for hunting. If you bathe your dog too often, it will reduce the special fat, which will make him more susceptible to the elements.

If you rescued an adult Dachshund, it may take a little while to get the dog used to being brushed frequently. If you aren't able to get your dog to feel comfortable with the brushing in the beginning, you can work it into your schedule, like training.

Short-haired Coat

The easiest of the three coats to maintain, your short-haired Dachshund will only need to be brushed about once a week. During the spring and fall, you may want to brush him a couple of times a week because he will be shedding more often, not that it will necessarily be noticeable since his hairs are so short.

Long-Haired Coat

Long-haired coats are the hardest to maintain, and daily brushing is pretty much essential to ensure that mats don't get out of control. The daily brushings don't need to take long, just enough to make sure that there aren't any tangles forming as those can quickly become mats in your dog's fur. Use the slicker brush for the daily brushing.

Start at your dog's head and work down his long body to make sure you get all of the tangles out.

Once a week, you will need to do a longer grooming session. This will require a second brushing with the bristled brush once you finish using the slicker brush. During this second round, look for tangles and be careful about how you brush them out as you don't want to hurt your Dachshund.

You will need to cut some of the hair every week as well. This will likely take a second person as your Dachshund may not want to sit still for a haircut. However, keeping the hair around his paws, ears, and underside clipped will keep the areas from tangling and matting as much.

Getting it just right can be tricky with the long-haired dogs. If you feel that it will help, you can go to a professional groomer a few times to see how the more detailed brushing and trimming is done. Ask questions so that you can take over after a couple of weeks – you won't have to keep going to the groomer, but a couple of trips can be very beneficial to you and your dog.

Wire-haired Coat

The wire-haired Dachshund sheds less than the other two breeds, and requires brushing once every couple of weeks (twice a month is fine). You may want to brush your little guy more often in spring and fall when he tends to shed more.

The reason why this Dachshund's coat is wiry is because it has a soft underlayer coat. During spring and fall, this layer will need to be stripped to remove the excess shedding. After a regular brushing, use a strip comb to remove the extra shedding from the second coat.

Senior Dogs

You can brush your senior dog more often if you would like, as the extra affection and time with you will likely be welcome. After all, he's slowing down, and just relaxing with you will be enjoyable (as well as your warmth feeling really good on his aging body). Grooming sessions are a good time to check for issues while giving your older pup a nice massage to ease any pain, as well as being a great way of having dedicated time together. While brushing your dog, look for any changes to the skin, such as bumps or fatty lumps. These may need to be mentioned to the vet during a regular visit if the bumps or lumps are very large.

Allergies

If your Dachshund is suffering from hot spots or if you notice his coat thinning out during grooming sessions, watch for these other problems, which could be a sign of allergies:

- Wounds take longer to heal

- Weak immune system

- Aching joints

- Hair is falling out

- Ear infections

Regular brushing ensures that you are more aware of the state of your Dachshund's coat, which can help you more quickly identify when your little dear is suffering from allergies. If you notice these issues, take your Dachshund to the vet.

Bath Time

Regardless of his coat length, your Dachshund will only need a bath about once a quarter (once every three months), unless he gets really dirty. Avoid washing him too often as his coat needs the natural oils that keep his fur looking shiny and healthy.

Of course, if your Dachshund gets dirty (which may happen whenever you go out exploring or hiking), then you'll need to take the time to bathe your canine after each of these events. Make sure the water isn't too cold or too hot, but comfortably warm. Make sure you don't get his head wet. Washing your dog's face is covered in the next section.

You can use these practices with other kinds of bathing, such as outside or at a public washing facility, modifying them to the tools you have at hand.

The first few times you bathe your dog, pay attention to the things that bother or scare him. If he is afraid of running water, make sure you

STEPS FOR BATH TIME

1 **GET EVERYTHING YOU WILL NEED IN ONE PLACE**
Make sure you have the following supplies ready: shampoo and conditioner (made for dogs), one large cup, towels, brush, non-slip tub mat.

2 **TAKE YOUR DACHSHUND OUT FOR A WALK.**
This will both tire your dog and make him a little hotter, which will make
the bath less hated – maybe even appreciated.

3 **RUN THE WATER**
Make sure that the temperature is lukewarm but not hot, especially if you
have just finished a walk. If you are washing him in a bathtub, you only
need enough water to cover up to your pup's stomach.

4 **TALK IN A STRONG CONFIDENT VOICE**
Don't use baby talk. Your Dachshund needs a confident leader, not to be
treated like an infant.

5 **PLACE THE DOG IN THE TUB**
and use the cup to wash the dog. Don't use too much soap – it isn't necessary. You can fully soak the dog starting at the neck and going to the
rump. It is fine to get him wet all at once, then to suds him up, or you can
do it a bit at a time if your dog is very wiggly. Just make sure that you don't get any
water on his head.

6 **TALK TO YOUR DOG**
while you are bathing him, keeping in mind you need to talk with confidence, not a high tone.

7 **MAKE SURE YOU DON'T GET WATER IN YOUR DOG'S EYES OR EARS**
You don't need to get water on the top of your dog's head. Use a wet
hand and gently scrub around his eyes and ears, being careful to avoid
getting soap or water in either. Follow the steps in the next section to
properly – and carefully – wash your dog's face and very long ears.

8 **RINSE OFF AGAINST THE GRAIN**
Make sure rinse the water up against the natural lay of the fur so that
there isn't any shampoo left beneath the hairs.

9 **TOWEL DRY AND BRUSH**
Toweling drying and rushing are great bonding times, towel dry and then
brush gently so your Dachshund enjoys the process and is excited for
the next bath!

10 **GIVE HIM A TREAT**
If he was particularly upset about the bath.

don't have the water running when your dog is in the tub. If he moves a lot when you start to apply the shampoo, it could indicate the smell is too strong. You need to modify the process to make it as comfortable for your dog as possible.

Keep in mind that you have to be patient and calm during the bath. If you get upset or take out your frustration on your dog, it will make all future baths that much more difficult because your dog will begin to stop trusting you. This isn't a fight for dominance, it is an honest lack of understanding for why you are torturing your dog when he already does so much to clean himself (from his standpoint). Keep a calm, loving tone as you wash your dog to make it a little easier next time. Sure, your Dachshund may whine, throw a tantrum, or wiggle excessively, but the better you take it, the more the dog will learn that bathing is simply a part of being in the pack.

If you have a long-haired Dachshund, some Dachshund enthusiasts recommend using a blow-dryer to speed up the drying process. Use the lowest setting to do this, and brush the fur as you regularly would as you blow dry your dog's long hair. Make sure you don't leave the heat in one area for long to avoid drying out your dog's skin.

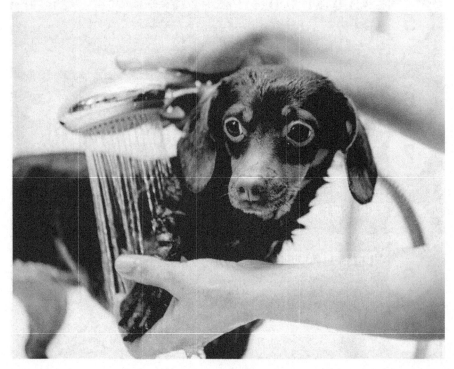

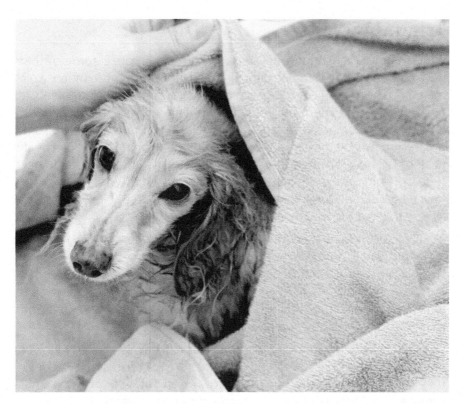

Cleaning Eyes And Ears

Use a washcloth to wash your dog's face and ears. When you bathe your Dachshund, be careful not to get water in his ears. You should also make a habit of checking his ears once a week to make sure they're healthy. He may have allergies that make the inside of his ears look red. A warm, moist pad can be used on the surface part of the ear. If the redness doesn't look better in a day, make an appointment to visit the vet. If you see wax buildup, you can very gently wipe it away. Never put anything in your dog's ears.

Dachshunds have several genetic eye conditions (Chapter 16), so take the time to always check your dog's eyes while you are grooming him. Cataracts are a fairly common problem for all dogs as they age. If you see cloudy eyes, have your Dachshund checked. If he's developing cataracts, you may need to take the pup in to have them removed because cataracts can lead to blindness.

Trimming Nails

Cutting a Dachshund's nails can be difficult because some of them have black nails and it can be difficult to tell how much is too much, which means that you may cut too much off and cause the quick to bleed. It's best to have an expert cut your dog's nails until you can see how it's done. If you have not cut a dog's nails before, you need to learn from a professional as the nails can bleed a lot if done wrong. Since it can be difficult to tell how far to go while trimming a Dachshund's nails, you need to learn from an expert before you try it yourself. If you already know how to cut a dog's nails, make sure to have some styptic powder nearby in case you cut too much nail off.

If you want to do it yourself, there are nail grinders that can help you to keep the nails trim without worrying about cutting them to the quick. However, if you use them, you will need to make sure that you don't grind too much off the nail. Seek help from a professional before you try to make sure you know how to use the grinder, keep your dog quiet, and make sure that it is done safely.

To know when your pup needs his nails cut, pay attention when your dog is walking on hard surfaces to make sure his nails aren't clicking. If they are, then you should increase how often you get your dog's nails trimmed. As a general rule, once a month is recommended.

Oral Health And Brushing Your Dog's Teeth

"I educate new owners the importance of getting their puppy used to having your fingers in their mouths and the taste of a good pet toothpaste. At least a couple times a week, rub some toothpaste on their teeth. People tend to forget the mouths but health issues can occur if mouths are not cared for properly by preventive measures that are so easy to do at home."

Kim Gillet
Cameo Dachshunds

Dachshunds need their teeth brushed daily to reduce dental problems as they tend to have problems with their teeth and gums. You prob-

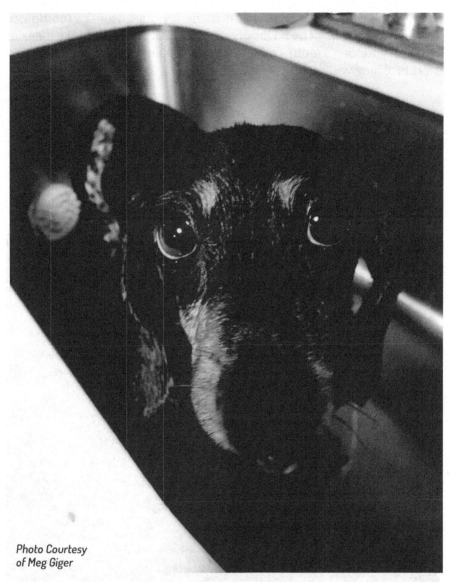

*Photo Courtesy
of Meg Giger*

ably will want to learn to do it yourself over having to visit a shop once a week. It's also nice to know how to brush your dog's teeth if his breath smells bad or he eats something that smells foul.

Again, you have to learn to be patient and keep it from being an all-out fight with your dog. It is a little weird, and your Dachshund may not be terribly happy with someone putting stuff in his mouth. However, once he is accustomed to it, the task will likely only take a few minutes a day.

Always use a toothpaste that is made for dogs. Human toothpaste can be toxic to dogs. The flavor of dog toothpaste will also make it easier to brush your dog's teeth – or at least entertaining as he tries to eat it. To start brushing your pup's teeth:

5

STEPS FOR FINGER BRUSHING YOUR DACHSHUND'S TEETH

1 GET YOUR DACHSHUND COMFORTABLE
Put a little toothpaste on your finger and let your Dachshund sniff and lick it. Once they do, praise them for trying something new!

2 POSITION YOUR PUP FOR EASY CONTROL
In an either sitting or kneeling position, Place your Dachshund in between your legs with his head facing away from you. This will allow you to control him as he squirms at first.

3 BRUSH IN SMALL CIRCLES AROUND EACH TOOTH
After reapplying toothpaste to your finger, lift up your dog's upper lip, and begin to rub in circles around your Dachshund's teeth. Your pup will likely make it difficult by constantly trying to lick your finger. Give your puppy praise when he doesn't wiggle too much. Try to move in a circular motion around each tooth, this will be hard with the smaller sharper teeth!

4 MASSAGE THE GUMS
Try to massage both the top and bottom gums. It is likely that the first few times you won't be able to do much more than get your finger in your dog's mouth, and that's okay. Over time, your puppy will learn to listen as training elsewhere helps your dog understand when you are giving commands

5 STAY POSITIVE
No, you probably won't be able to clean the puppy's teeth properly for a while, and that is perfectly fine so long as you keep working at it patiently and consistently.

Once your dog seems all right with you brushing his teeth with your finger, try the same steps with a canine toothbrush. It may be a similar song and dance in the beginning, but it shouldn't take nearly as long for him to accept the toothbrush. It could take a couple of weeks before you can graduate to a toothbrush.

CHAPTER 15
General Health Issues: Allergies, Parasites, And Vaccinations

Because of their short stature, you need to be very careful of the environmental factors that your Dachshund is exposed to every day. He is going to love going out to new places and hiking in forests – that is what he was bred to do. You don't want to deny him the things he loves; however, you do need to make sure that your excursions don't exacerbate any environmental allergies your dog might have, and you will have to monitor him for parasites. For example, if you live near a wooded area, your dog is at a greater risk of ticks than a dog that lives in the city. Talk to your vet about particular environmental risks to your dog.

Photo Courtesy of Jen Cherry

The Role Of Your Veterinarian

From getting annual vaccines updated to health checkups, regularly scheduled vet visits will make sure that your Dachshund stays healthy. If your Dachshund seems sluggish or less excited than usual, it could be a sign that there is something wrong with him. Fortunately, the breed's outgoing personality tends to make it easy to tell when a dog isn't feeling well. Annual visits to the vet will ensure there isn't a problem that is slowly draining the energy or health from your dog.

Health checkups also make sure that your Dachshund is aging well. If there are any early symptoms of something potentially wrong with your dog over the years (such as arthritis), an early diagnosis will allow you to start making adjustments early. The vet can help you come up with ways to manage pain and problems that come with the aging process and will be able to recommend adjustments to the schedule to accommodate your canine's aging body and diminishing abilities. This will ensure that you can keep having fun together without hurting your dog.

Vets can provide treatments and/or preventive medications for the different parasites and microscopic threats that your dog may encounter when he is outside, during interactions with other dogs, or from exposure to animals outside your home.

Allergies

Dachshunds aren't known for having allergies, but some of them do have allergic reactions to their environment (not just food). They usually don't have the same kind of reaction as people though. Instead of sneezing, coughing, and runny noses, allergies often present as skin irritations. This is easier to spot on a short-haired Dachshund than the other two types as you will probably see the irritation, and it will definitely be easy to see if your dog has been chewing on one area of his body more often than others.

The scientific name for environmental allergies is atopic dermatitis, but it's more difficult to tell whether the problem is with the environment or the food you're giving your dog. The symptoms tend to be similar in dogs for both types of allergies:

- Itching/scratching, particularly around the face
- Hot spots
- Ear infections
- Skin infections
- Runny eyes and nose (not as common)

Grooming your dog is a great time to pay attention to many of these potential problems.

Dogs often develop allergies when they are between 1 and 5 years old. Once they develop an allergy, canines don't outgrow the problem. Usually dog allergies are related to skin exposure, but some canines can be allergic to inhaling microscopic particles, such as dust, molds, and pollens.

Since the symptoms are the same for food and environmental allergies, you will need to talk to your vet about determining the cause. If your dog has a food allergy, all you have to do is change the food that you give him. If he has an environmental allergy, he will need medication, just as humans do. Because of this, you will want to know if the problem is from something seasonal (like pollen) or something year round so you will know when to treat your dog.

As with humans, completely eliminating the problem really isn't reasonable – there is only so much you can do to change the environment around your dog. There are several types of medications that can help your dog become less sensitive to the allergens.

- **Antibacterials/Antifungals** – Shampoos, pills, and creams usually do not treat the allergy but the underlying problems that come with allergies, such as bacterial and yeast infections.

- **Anti-inflammatories** – These are over-the-counter oral medications that are comparable to allergy medicine for people. You will need to be careful if you use these medications, monitoring your dog to see if he has any adverse effects. Don't start to give your dog any medication without first consulting with the vet. If your dog has a bad reaction, such as lethargy, diarrhea, or dehydration you should consult with your vet.

- **Immunotherapy** – A series of shots can help reduce your dog's sensitivity to whatever he is allergic to. This is something you can do at home, so you won't need to take your dog to the vet to complete the series. Learn how to give the shots from your vet, and then you can find out how to give the shots for the environmental problems in your area. Scientists are also developing an oral version of the medication to make it easier to take care of your dog.

- **Topical** – This medication tends to be a type of shampoo and conditioner that will remove any allergens from your dog's fur. Giving your dog a warm (not hot) bath can also help relieve itching.

Talk with your vet about the medications that are available for your dog to determine the best treatment for your situation and your Dachshund's needs.

Inhalant And Environmental Allergies

Inhalant allergies are caused by things like dust, pollen, mold, and even dog dander. Your dog might scratch at a particular hot spot or he might start to paw at his eyes and ears. Some dogs have runny noses and sneeze prolifically, but this is usually in addition to scratching.

Contact Allergies

Contact allergies mean that your dog has touched something that triggers an allergic reaction. Things like wool, chemicals in a flea treatment, and certain grasses can trigger irritation in a dog's skin, even causing discoloration. If left untreated, the allergic reaction can cause the affected area to emit strong odors and cause fur loss.

Like food allergies, contact allergies are easy to treat because once you know what is irritating your dog's skin, you can remove the problem.

Fleas And Ticks

Dachshunds tend to love being outside (except when the weather doesn't suit them), so you will need to be very careful about fleas and ticks. Even in your backyard, fleas are a problem nearly year round. Neither parasite is easy to see because of the darker coloring most Dachshunds tend to have. You can't allow any lapse in anti-flea and tick treatment, even in the winter.

Make it a habit to check for ticks after every outing into the woods, or near long grass or wild plants. Comb through your dog's fur and check his skin for irritation and parasites. Since you will be doing this often, you should be able to notice when there's a change, such as a new bump, for example. Since your dog will be very happy to spend time with you, the skin check shouldn't take long.

Fleas are problematic because they're far more mobile than ticks. The best way to look for fleas is to make it a regular part of your brushing sessions. There is a flea comb that you can use. If you see black specks on the comb after brushing through your dog's fur, this could be a sign of fleas. Instead of using a comb, you can put your dog on a white towel and run your hand over the fur. Fleas and flea dirt are likely to fall on the towel. Fleas often are seen on the stomach, so you may notice them

Photo Courtesy of Anna Tolley

when your pup wants a belly rub. You can also look for behavioral indicators, such as incessant scratching and licking. You will need to use flea preventative products on a regular basis once your puppy reaches an appropriate age.

Along with being annoying, both can carry parasites and illnesses that can be passed on to you and your dog. Ticks notoriously carry Lyme disease, which can be debilitating or deadly if untreated. Lyme disease symptoms include headaches, fever, and fatigue. The bite itself often has a red circle around it that may grow. Since your dog will likely start to act sluggish after you find a tick attached to his skin, make sure to look for the circular rash, and if you see one or aren't sure, go to the vet to have it checked.

If the tick hasn't latched on, you can just remove it. If a tick hasn't latched on, then it hasn't bitten your dog. Ticks will fall off your dog once they are full, so if you find a tick on your dog, it will either be looking to latch onto your dog or it will be feeding. Use the following steps to remove the tick if it has latched onto your dog.

1. Apply rubbing alcohol to the area where the tick is.

2. Use tweezers to pull the tick off of your dog. Do not use your fingers because infections are transmitted through blood, and you don't want it to latch onto you.

3. Examine the spot where the tick was to make sure it is fully removed. Sometimes the head will remain, so you will need to make sure all of the tick is gone.

4. Set up a meeting with the vet to have it checked.

The FDA has issued a warning about some store-bought treatments. Whether you look into purchasing treatments that have to be applied monthly or a collar for constant protection, you need to check the treatment to see if it contains isoxazoline (included in Bravecto, Nexgard, Credelio, and Simparica) because this ingredient can have an adverse effect on some pets. While other ingredients are safe for pets when used in the proper doses, if you use a product that is meant for a larger dog, it can be toxic to your dog. Consult with your vet about recommended treatments to ensure that you get the right dose of flea and tick repellant for your dog's size and needs. When you start applying the treatment, monitor your dog for the following issues:

- Diarrhea/vomiting

*Photo Courtesy
of Vickie Rich*

- Trembling
- Lethargy
- Seizures

Take your dog to the vet if you notice any of these issues.

Never use any product designed for a dog on a cat or vice versa. If your dog is sick, pregnant, or nursing, you may need to look for an alternative treatment. Flea collars are generally not recommended because they are known to cause problems in pets and people. If you have a cat or young children, you should choose one of the other options for keeping fleas and ticks off of your dog. This is because flea collars contain an ingredient that is lethal to felines and which might be carcinogenic to humans.

When you purchase a flea treatment, make sure to read the packaging to find out when is the right time to begin treating your dog based on his current age and size. Different brands have different recommendations, and you don't want to start treating your puppy too early. There are also very important steps to apply the treatment. Make sure you understand all of the steps before you purchase the flea treatment.

If you want to use natural products instead of chemical ones, set aside a few hours to research the alternatives and find out what works best for your Dachshund. Verify that any natural products work before you buy them and make sure you consult with your vet. Establishing a regular schedule and adding it to the calendar will help you remember to consistently treat your dog each month.

Parasitic Worms

Although worms are a less common problem than fleas and ticks, they can be far more dangerous. Your dog can become sick from worms that are carried by fleas and ticks. There are a number of types of worms that you should be aware of:

- Heartworms
- Hookworms
- Roundworms
- Tapeworms

- Whipworms

Unfortunately, there isn't an easy-to-recognize set of symptoms to help identify when your dog has worms. However, you can keep an eye out for these symptoms, and if your dog shows them, schedule a visit to the vet.

- Your Dachshund is unexpectedly lethargic for at least a few days.

- Patches of fur begin to fall out (this will be noticeable if you brush your Dachshund regularly) or if you notice patchy spaces in your dog's coat.

- Your dog's stomach becomes distended (expands) and looks like a potbelly.

- Your Dachshund begins coughing, vomiting, has diarrhea, or has a loss in appetite.

If you aren't sure about any symptom, it's always best to get to the vet as soon as possible.

Heartworms

Heartworms are a significant threat to your dog's health and can be deadly as they can both slow and stop blood flow. As such, you should consistently treat your dog with heartworm protection.

Fortunately, heartworms are among the easiest health problems to prevent. There are medications that can ensure your Dachshund does not get heartworms. To prevent this very serious problem, you can give your dog a chewable medication, topical medicine, or you can request shots.

This particular parasite is carried by mosquitoes, which are nearly impossible to avoid in most regions of the country. Since heartworms are potentially deadly, taking preventative measures is essential.

If a dog has heartworms, the condition is costly and time-consuming to treat and cure, but it will be well worth all of the work to keep your pup healthy and happy.

1. The vet will draw blood to conduct tests, which can cost as much as $1,000.

2. Treatment will begin with some initial medications, including antibiotics and anti-inflammatory drugs.

3. Following a month of the initial medication, your vet will give your dog three shots over the course of two months.

From the time when the vet confirms that your dog has heartworms until he or she says your dog is clear of the parasite, you have to keep your dog calm. Your vet will tell you how best to exercise your canine during this time. Considering your Dachshund is likely to be energetic, this is going to be a very rough time for both you and your dog. You will need to be careful when your dog exercises because the worms are in your dog's heart, inhibiting blood flow. Therefore, getting your dog's heart pumping too much can kill him.

Treatment will continue after the shots are complete. After about 6 months, your vet will conduct another blood test to ensure that the worms are gone.

Once your dog is cleared of the parasites, you will need to be vigilant about medicating your dog against heartworms. You want to make sure that your poor little guy doesn't suffer through that again. There will be lasting damage to your dog's heart, so you will need to ensure that your dog does not over exercise.

Intestinal Worms: Hookworms, Roundworms, Tapeworms, And Whipworms

All four of these worms thrive in your dog's intestinal tract, and they get there when your dog eats something contaminated with them. The following are the most common ways that dogs ingest worms:

- Feces
- Small hosts, such as fleas, cockroaches, earthworks, and rodents
- Soil, including licking it from their fur and paws
- Contaminated water
- Mother's milk (if the mother has worms, she can pass it to young puppies when they nurse)

The following are the most common symptoms and problems caused by intestinal parasites:

- Anemia
- Blood loss
- Coughing
- Dehydration
- Diarrhea

- Large intestine inflammation

- Weight loss

If a dog rests in soil with hookworm larvae, the parasite can burrow through the canine's skin. Vets will conduct a diagnostic test to determine if your dog has this parasite. If your dog does have hookworms, your vet will prescribe a de-wormer. You should visit a doctor yourself because humans can get hookworms, too.

Roundworms are kind of like fleas in that they are very common, and at some point in their lives, most dogs have to be treated for them. They primarily eat the digested food in your dog's stomach, getting the nutrients that your dog needs. It is possible for larvae to remain in your dog even after all of the adult worms have been eradicated. Mothers can pass these larvae to their puppies. This means if you have a pregnant Dachshund, you will need to have her puppies periodically checked to make sure the inactive larvae aren't passed on to the puppies. The mother will also need to go through the same testing to make sure the worms don't make her sick. In addition to the symptoms listed above, your Dachshund may appear to have a potbelly. You may also see the worms in your dog's excrement or vomit.

Tapeworms are usually eaten when they are eggs, usually carried by fleas or from the feces of other animals that have tapeworms. They develop in the canine's small intestine until they are adults. Over time, parts of the tapeworm will break off and become obvious in your dog's waste, which needs to be carefully cleaned up to keep other animals from getting tapeworms. While tapeworms typically aren't fatal, they can cause weight loss while giving your dog a potbelly (depending on how big the worms grow to be in your dog's intestines).

Your vet can test your dog to see if he has tapeworms, and will prescribe a medication that you can give your dog, including chewables, tablets, or a medication you can sprinkle on your dog's food. There is a low risk of humans getting tapeworms, with kids being at the greatest risk because of the likelihood that they will play in areas where there is dog waste and then not wash their hands carefully enough afterward. It is possible to contract tapeworms if a person swallows a flea, which is possible if your dog and home have a serious infestation.

Whipworms grow in the large intestine, and in large numbers they can be fatal. Their name is indicative of their appearance, with their tails appearing thinner than the upper section. Like the other worms, you will need to have your dog tested to determine if he is sick.

Keeping up with flea treatments, making sure people pick up behind their pets, and watching to make sure your Dachshund doesn't eat trash or animal waste are the best preventative measures to keep your dog safe from getting these parasites.

If your dog has hookworms or roundworms, these can be spread to you from your dog through skin contact. Being treated at the same time as your Dachshund can help stop the vicious cycle of continually switching which of you has worms.

Preventative measures against all of these worms can be included with the preventative medication for heartworms. Talk to your vet about the different options to keep your pet from suffering any of these health problems.

Vaccinating Your Dachshund

Vaccination schedules are almost universal for all dog breeds, including Dachshunds. The following list can help you ensure your Dachshund receives the necessary shots on schedule. Make sure to add this to your calendar. As a reminder, no shots should be administered during your puppy's very first vet visit. Your new dog already has enough stress with all of the changes in his life. If your puppy is due for more shots soon after arriving at your home, that trip should be scheduled separately, once your puppy feels more comfortable in your home. Until your puppy has finished vaccinations, you should be avoiding dogs outside of your home, and keeping exposure to your other dogs to a minimum.

HELPFUL TIP
Staying Healthy

Dachshunds are prone to bacterial and viral infections. Talk to your veterinarian about appropriate vaccinations for your pet. Daily brushing and yearly checkups by your veterinarian can prevent dental diseases, such as tartar buildup and gum infection.

The following table provides details on which shots should be administered and when.

Timeline	Shot		
6 to 8 weeks	Bordetella Lyme	Leptospira Influenza Virus-H3N8	DHPP – First shot Influenza Virus-H3N2
10 to 12 weeks	Leptospira Lyme	DHPP – Second shot Influenza Virus-H3N8	Rabies Influenza Virus-H3N2
14 to 16 weeks	DHPP – Third shot		
Annually	Leptospira Lyme	Bordetella Influenza Virus-H3N8	Rabies Influenza Virus-H3N2
Every 3 Years	DHPP Booster	Rabies (if opted for longer duration vaccination)	

These shots protect your dog against a range of ailments. Keep in mind that you will need to make shots an annual part of your dog's vet visits so that you can continue to keep your pup safe. If you would like to learn more about the diseases these vaccinations protect your dog from contracting, check out the Canine Journal. They provide details about the ailments and other information that can help you understand why it is so important to keep up with the shots.

Holistic Alternatives

Wanting to keep a dog from a lot of exposure to chemical treatments makes sense, and there are many good reasons why people are moving to more holistic methods. However, doing this requires a lot more research and monitoring to ensure that the methods are working – and, most importantly, do not harm your dog. Unverified holistic medicines can be a waste of money, or, worse, they can even be harmful to your pet.

If you decide to go with holistic medication, talk with your vet about your options. You can also seek out Dachshund experts to see what they recommend before you start using any methods you are interested in trying. Read what scientists have said about the medicine you are considering. There is a chance that the more generic products you buy from a store are actually better than some holistic medications sold in specialty stores.

Make sure you are thorough in your research and that you don't take any unnecessary risks with the health of your Dachshund. Things like acupuncture are popular, but these treatments don't have the same effects on dogs as they do on humans. With many sites dedicated to taking care of Dachshunds, you can find some information on what is recommended. It is possible that something like massage therapy can do a lot to help your dog, especially as he ages. You will need to be careful though because of the potential health problems the breed has. Follow the recommendations on the reputable Dachshund sites to provide the best, safest care for your dog. There is even a special type of chiropractic therapy for dogs, but you will need to be careful about finding a reputable chiropractor for your pup so that the chiropractor doesn't do more harm than good.

CHAPTER 16
Genetic Health Concerns Common To The Dachshund

"Dachshunds are known for having delicate spines. There seems to be a genetic correlation to IVDD. Keeping your Dachshund at a healthy weight and not allowing them to jump from high spaces will help protect his spine."

Elizabeth Bender
BenderDachs

Apart from their proclivity for back injuries, Dachshunds are surprisingly healthy purebred canines. That doesn't mean that they don't have genetic issues, and several of the potential issues are serious. This is why it is so important to research the breeder before you adopt a puppy. Good breeders offer guarantees (Chapter 3) to ensure their puppies can be returned if they have one of a particular breed's known genetic issues. To meet the requirements of these guarantees you have to know the problems and their symptoms. The sooner you start to counter any potential problems, the healthier your Dachshund is likely to be.

HELPFUL TIP
Health Risks

Dachshunds, like all purebred dogs, are prone to certain health issues. Because of their short legs, Doxies are associated with Intervertebral Disc Disease (IVDD). They may also have eye issues such as Progressive Retinal Atrophy (PRA), Cushing's Disease, diabetes, or hypothyroidism. All dogs have health issues, especially purebreds. Offense is the best defense regarding health care for your pet.

Breeders should be able to provide health records in addition to any shot records and required tests. Making sure that the parents are healthy increases the likelihood that your puppy will remain healthy over the course of his entire life. However, there is still a chance that your dog will have one of these documented problems even if the parents don't, so you will need to keep an eye on your little friend.

Intervertebral Disc Disease

Because of their geneti-
cally long backs, Dachshunds
are prone to spinal injuries.
Intervertebral disc disease (IVDD)
is a genetic disease that causes
the discs and vertebrae to become brittle. This disease coupled with the long back makes it
more likely that your Dachshund
will sustain a ruptured or slipped
discs, especially as he ages. This
can lead to permanent damage
to your Dachshund's spine, and,
in the worst cases, it can leave
your poor pup paralyzed.

Photo Courtesy
of Jennifer Henderson

Though it has been covered
in earlier chapters, to help you
to ensure that your Dachshund
does not hurt his back, especially
if he has IVDD, here is a reminder of the things you can do to reduce the risk of injury to your
dog's spine.

- Make sure that he gets enough exercise, keeping him at a
  healthy weight.

- As much as possible, keep your Dachshund from jumping off things,
  particularly furniture and in/out of your car. The effort to jump from
  such a low place coupled with the impact when they hit the ground
  can harm your dog's back.

- If at any point you have to pick up your dog (such as due to an injury, aggressive larger animal, or unexpectedly steep stairs when you
  are exploring with your dog), make sure that you pick up both ends
  of your dog at one time – do not lift your dog up under the front paws
  alone. You do not want the lower part of your dog to swing like a pen-
  dulum when you lift him off the ground. Make sure that you keep his
  full body – both the front and back half – supported for as long as you
  are holding your dog.

Acanthosis Nigricans

Despite how bad the disease name sounds, this genetic disease isn't deadly. It causes your dog's skin to become abnormally dark. There are two types of the condition, and Dachshunds suffer from the first type (and they are nearly the only breed that does – it is incredibly rare).

If your Dachshund has this disease, it will present over the first year. His skin will begin to get darker and thicker. This can cause bacterial or yeast infections over the affected parts of the dog's skin. It isn't life threatening, but treatment is usually done through injections and medicinal shampoos.

Photo Courtesy of Deborah Swingley

It is rare, and typically vets will take a biopsy to determine if a Dachshund has this disease.

The other form of the disease is caused by friction when a dog is obese or has some physical abnormalities. It could also be an indication of something more serious, such as hyperthyroidism or another kind of hormonal imbalance. Allergies can also contribute to the second form of Acanthosis Nigricans. Since this type is often caused by an outside issue, treatment is much more straightforward, including treating the underlying issue. If a case is severe, injections may be required.

Whatever the cause, you need to consult a vet if you notice darker areas of your dog's skin so that the condition can be treated.

Hypothyroidism

This is a problem that is also found in humans (and many other dog breeds). Hypothyroidism is a result of the sufferer's body not making enough thyroid hormone. It often begins to show in Dachshunds between two and six years old, and symptoms include weight gain, lack of energy, and skin problems (such as dry or itchy skin).

A blood test is done to find out if a Dachshund has hypothyroidism. Some vets will conduct the test annually as a preventative measure. If your dog has hypothyroidism, your vet will likely prescribe oral medication.

Cushing's Disease

Also known as hyperadrenocorticism, this disease is a result of a dog's adrenal glands producing excess amounts of the hormone cortisone. It is easy to mistake this disease as a result of aging. Symptoms of hyperadrenocorticism include drinking excessively, using the bathroom more often, loss of appetite and hair, and gaining weight.

If you notice your dog gaining weight, drinking more, or having accidents around the home, take him to the vet. Make sure to mention the problems you've noticed so they can do an analysis for Cushing's disease. It is treatable, so the earlier you catch it, the better your dog's quality of life will be. Treatment usually includes medication, though in the worst cases it may require surgery.

Dental Issues

Dachshunds are notorious for their dental issues. Part of the problem is that their teeth may overcrowd their small mouths, which increases how much food is trapped between the teeth. This causes the formation of more plaque, which can lead to gum inflammation and infection.

To keep your dog's mouth healthy, you need to make sure you regularly brush his teeth. This may occasionally include taking him to a professional for a more thorough cleaning, though you will need to find a professional who can do it without using anesthesia. Because of their size, Dachshunds should not be given anesthesia as it can kill them. If you regularly brush your dog's teeth, you should be able to help keep your dog's mouth fairly healthy.

Cardiac Disorders

One of the two more worrisome disorders common to Dachshunds this cute little breed tends to suffer from is degenerative mitral valve disease. When a dog has this problem, a heart valve leaks, and it typically starts when the dog is in the golden years, between 8 and 10 years old. You want to make sure your Dachshund is checked for this issue as he gets older. When caught early, the issues can be minimized through medication. Keeping your dog at a healthy weight is important to keep his heart from overworking.

Brain Disorders

The second concerning problem relates to the Dachshund's brain. There are several problems that are more common in Dachshunds than most other breeds.

- Dachshunds may suffer from narcolepsy. They will be more lethargic and any strong emotional trigger may cause them to fall asleep. There is no warning as to when your dog will pass out either. It could be excitement about a car ride or treat. Perhaps you left a door open, causing your Dachshund to get overexcited about escaping. There is no treatment.

- Lafora disease is a more severe type of epilepsy that presents as strong muscle jerks. The seizures usually only last for a couple of seconds. This is a problem most common with miniature wire-haired Dachshunds.

If you notice either of these problems, or any other kind of seizure or indications of a neurological disorder, take your dog to the vet as quickly as possible.

Eye Issues

Those adorable large eyes in the small face of a Dachshund are beautiful, but they also can have a lot of problems. Many of these problems are not common, but you should monitor your pup so you can get treatment as early as possible. Several of these conditions can result in blindness if left untreated.

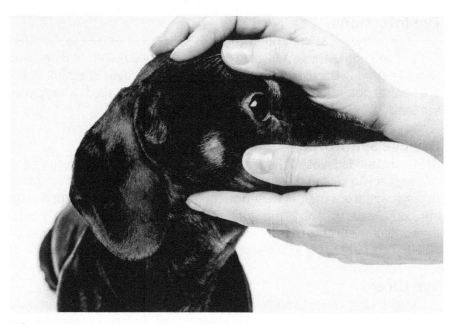

Glaucoma

A painful eye ailment, glaucoma can result in blindness if it isn't treated early. If you notice your Dachshund's eyes watering a lot, the cornea turning blue, or your dog squinting often, get him to the vet. These are signs that your dog is in pain, which can be difficult to notice because you get accustomed to the behavior.

You can also have your vet do an annual glaucoma screening. This will help you know that your dog is alright.

Progressive Retinal Atrophy (Pra)

PRA causes light sensitivity because of problems with the retina. Puppies should be tested, so if you adopt your puppy from a breeder, you should have a guarantee against this particular problem.

Dogs with this condition usually start presenting with night blindness, which can make your dog more nervous. If you look at your dog's eyes, they may also reflect light more as the eyes deteriorate. The ailment affects both eyes, so the problem should show in both.

There is no treatment for the condition. You will need to learn to accommodate your dog's failing sight over time.

Eye Infections

One of the most common problems for Dachshunds' eyes is infections. If you notice those adorable eyes start to look red or inflamed, you should get your Dachshund to the vet to have his eyes checked. There are several potential causes for the problems, so you need to have your vet check the eyes to determine how to treat the problem.

Dry Eye Syndrome

Dachshunds' eyes may have reduced tear production, resulting in dry eyes. It can cause your dog to scratch at his eyes or mucus may start to discharge from their eyes. If untreated, it can cause severe problems and complications, and in the worst case can result in blindness. To treat the condition, surgery may be required. If it isn't severe, your vet may be able to regularly apply artificial tears.

Eye Ulcers

Dachshunds tend to suffer from this problem more often than most breeds. Eye ulcers often appear suddenly, and they require immediate treatment to keep them from becoming worse. The following are the most common symptoms of this eye issue:

- Craters or holes that you can see on the eye's surface
- Red or inflamed eyes
- Weeping
- Excessive closing of the eyes and squinting

Usually, ulcers are caused by injury to those large eyes or the eyelids. They can also result from some of the other problems on this list, such as dry eye syndrome.

If treated quickly after forming, it will only take your dog a few days to recover.

Fungal Ear Infections

Dogs' ears can create a dark, warm place for fungus, yeast, and bacteria to thrive. With the Dachshund having particularly long ears that will have a tendency to flip inside out all the time, there is a risk that they will develop ear infections. Allergies can be a major contributing factor, but all dogs are at risk for these types of infections. This is why it is absolute-

*Photo Courtesy
of Lee Roberts
Roberts Twins Photography*

ly essential that you do not let your dog's ears get wet during bath time, and why you must monitor his ear health. Watch for the following issues in your dog's ears:

- Colored discharge (particularly brown or bloody)

- Swelling and redness

- Crust forming on the skin of the ear flap

- Scratching at the ear or frequent shaking of the head

- Loss of hearing or balance

- Walking in circles (beyond the usual for bathroom inspections or nesting before lying down)

If you notice any of these symptoms, take your dog to the vet, even if the symptoms seem mild. There are a number of different available treatments, depending on the severity of the condition. Usually an anti-fungal cream will be recommended, but more serious problems (such as an infection in the middle ear) could require injections or surgery.

If your dog suffers from chronic fungal ear infections, your vet will likely recommend an ear cleaner designed to prevent the problem or a solution that will keep the area dry.

Photo Courtesy of Robin Klein

Common Owner Mistakes

The two biggest potential problems are injuries to Dachshunds' backs and obesity, but they aren't the only things that could go wrong. In addition to genetic problems, there are things that you can do that could damage your dog's health related to diet and exercise levels. In the early days, it is a difficult balance to strike as your puppy is curious and enthusiastic. Even when he is a fully grown dog, you have to make sure that you are minimizing how much stress is placed on your Dachshund's frame. Weight management is one important way of keeping your dog healthy. You need to ensure that your dog is getting the right nutrition for his activity level to keep him from having a greater risk of exacerbating hip and elbow dysplasia.

Failing to notice early signs of potential issues can be detrimental, even fatal. If at any point you notice strange changes in your dog's behavior, take him to the vet. As a fairly healthy breed, strange behavior in a Dachshund is likely a sign of something that should be checked.

Prevention And Monitoring

The recent trend of "cute" overweight Dachshunds has called attention to the potential health risks that this kind of trend can cause. This is a breed that is already cute, and you should never sacrifice your dog's health in the name of cute. Instead, take extra time to train your dog to do something cute. This is both healthier and more fun for your little guy and you.

Checking your Dachshund's weight is important and should be done at least once a quarter or twice a year. Your vet will likely talk to you if your dog is overweight because this not only puts a strain on the dog's long back, legs, joints, and muscles, but it can also have adverse effects on your dog's heart, blood flow, and respiratory system. Make sure to talk to your vet if you notice that your Dachshund is having any trouble. Those regular vet visits can help you address issues that you may not think are that big a deal. Sometimes the symptoms you notice are a sign of a future problem.

Photo Courtesy
of Katrice Brown

CHAPTER 17
The Aging Dachshund

The average life expectancy of a Dachshund is between 12 and 16 years old, an age range that makes it one of the longer lived breeds. There have even been some Dachshunds that have lived to about two decades old. If you take good care of your Dachshund, you could be in for a long, loving partnership with your little pooch. Of course it will never seem like it is enough time, but there is a lot you can do to extend your dog's life. A Dachshund that is well taken care of will live longer if he doesn't have many significant health issues, which makes it all the more important to make sure your pup gets regular exercise and has a good diet. You want your Dachshund to live a long, happy life.

At some point you will notice that your Dachshund is slowing down, and that is a sign that your little buddy is starting to feel the age in his bones. This usually happens at around 9 or 10 years old. A dog may remain healthy his whole life, but his body still won't be able to do the same activities as the years start to take their toll. The changes that are necessary as your dog ages will be based on your Dachshund's specific needs.

The first signs of age are usually your dog's walking becoming a little stiffer or when he starts panting more heavily earlier in the walk. If you see that, start to tone back the long walks, and just go for more, shorter walks. Your Dachshund may want to continue to be active, which means you will need to ensure the activity levels don't stop, just make an adjustment in the kinds of activities you do.

Your schedule is going to need to change as your canine slows down. Be careful to ensure that your pup doesn't overexert himself if he tries to remain active. Your Dachshund may not want to accept that things are changing and he won't be able to control it.

There is a reason these are called the golden years – you can really enjoy them with your dog. You don't have to worry as much about him tearing things up out of boredom or getting overexcited on walks anymore. You can enjoy lazy evenings and peaceful weekends with some less strenuous exercise to break up the day. It's easy to make the senior years incredibly enjoyable for your Dachshund and yourself by making the necessary adjustments.

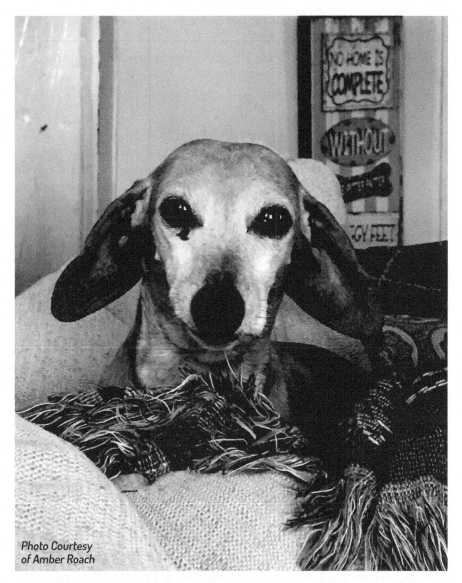

Photo Courtesy
of Amber Roach

Senior Care Challenges

In most cases, caring for an older dog is much simpler than taking care of a younger dog, and Dachshunds are no exception. With Dachshunds, you actually already have a head start since you've been working to keep your dog from injuring his back for years. It is possible that you may not need to do much to change your home for your aging pup.

Accommodations you should make for your senior Dachshund include:

- Set water bowls out in a couple of different places so that your dog can easily reach them as needed.

- Cover hard floor surfaces (such as tile, hardwood, and vinyl). Use non-slip carpets or rugs.

- Add cushions and softer bedding for your Dachshund. This will make the surface more comfortable. There are bed warmers for dogs if your Dachshund displays achy joints or muscles often. Of course, you also need to make sure he isn't too warm, so this can be a fine balancing act.

- To improve his circulation, increase how often you brush your Dachshund.

- Stay inside in extreme heat and cold. Your Dachshund is somewhat hardy, but an old canine cannot handle changes in temperature as well as he once did.

- Use stairs or ramps for your Dachshund (if you haven't already) so that the old pup doesn't have to try to jump.

- Avoid moving your furniture around, particularly if your Dachshund shows signs of having trouble with his sight or has dementia. A familiar home is more comforting and less stressful as your pet ages. If your Dachshund isn't able to see as clearly as he once did, keeping the home familiar will make it easier for your dog to move around without getting hurt.

- If you have stairs that your Dachshunds can no longer use, consider setting up an area where your dog can stay without having to go up and down them too often.

- Create a space where your Dachshund can relax with fewer distractions and noises. Don't make your old friend feel isolated, but do give him a place to get away from everyone if he needs to be alone.

- Be prepared to let your dog out more often for restroom breaks.

Common Physical Disorders Related To Aging

Previous chapters cover illnesses that are common or likely with a Dachshund, but old age tends to bring a slew of ailments that aren't particular to any one breed. Here are the things you will need to watch for (as well as talking to your vet about them).

*Photo Courtesy
of Tamara Hanson*

- Arthritis is probably the most common ailment in any dog breed, and the Dachshund is no exception. If your dog is showing signs of stiffness and pain after normal activities, talk with your vet about safe ways to help minimize the pain and discomfort of this common joint ailment.

- Gum disease is a common issue in older dogs as well, and you should be just as vigilant about brushing his teeth when your dog gets older as at any other age. A regular check of your Dachshund's teeth and gums can help ensure this does not become a problem.

- Loss of eyesight or blindness is relatively common in older dogs, just as it is in humans. Have your dog's vision checked at least once a year and more often if it is obvious that his eyesight is failing.

- Kidney disease is a common problem in older dogs, and one that you should monitor for the older your Dachshund gets. If your canine is drinking more often and having accidents regularly, get your Dachshund to the vet as soon as possible and have him checked for kidney disease.

- Diabetes is probably the greatest concern for a breed that loves to eat as much as your Dachshund does, even with daily exercise for most of the dog's adult life. Although diabetes is usually thought of as a genetic condition, any Dachshund can become diabetic if not fed and exercised properly. This is another reason why it's so important to be careful with your Dachshund's diet and exercise levels.

Steps, Ramps, And Wheelchairs

You shouldn't pick your Dachshund up to carry him upstairs or put him in the car – he still wants to have some independence, and you could be potentially doing damage when you lift him. Steps and ramps are the best way to safely ensure your Dachshund can maintain some level of self-sufficiency as he ages. Also, using steps and ramps provides a bit of extra exercise.

Vet Visits

As your Dachshund ages, you are going to notice the slow down, and the pain in your Dachshund's body will be obvious, just like it is in an older person. Make regular visits with your vet to ensure that you aren't doing anything that could potentially harm your Dachshund. If your Dachshund has a debilitating ailment or condition, you may want to dis-

Photo Courtesy of Gisela Benitez

cuss the options for ensuring a better quality of life for him, such as wheels if your Dachshund's legs begin to have serious issues.

The Importance Of Regular Vet Visits And What To Expect

Just as humans go to visit the doctor more often as they age, you'll need to take your dog to see your vet with greater frequency. The vet can make sure that your Dachshund is staying active without overdoing it, and that there is no unnecessary stress on your older dog. If your canine has sustained an injury and hidden it from you, your vet is more likely to detect it.

Your vet can also make recommendations about activities and changes to your schedule based on your Dachshund's physical abilities and any changes in personality. For example, if your Dachshund is panting more now, it could be a sign of pain from stiffness. Your vet can help you determine the best way to keep your Dachshund happy and active during the later years.

The following are the kinds of things to expect when you go to the vet.

- Your vet is going to talk about your dog's history, even if you have visited every year. This talk is necessary to see how things have gone or if any possible problems have started to manifest themselves or have gotten worse.

- While you chat, your vet will probably conduct a complete physical examination to assess your dog's health.

- Depending on how old your dog is and the kind of health he is in, your vet may want to run different tests. The following are some of the most common tests for older dogs.

  - Arthropod-borne disease testing, which involves drawing blood and testing it for viral infections

  - Chemistry Screening for kidney, liver, and sugar evaluation

  - Complete blood count

  - Fecal Flotation, which involves mixing your dog's poop with a special liquid to test for worms and other parasites

  - Heartworm testing

  - Urinalysis, which tests your dog's urine to check the health of your dog's kidneys and urinary system

- The routine wellness check that the vet has been conducting on your dog for years
- Any breed-specific tests for your aging Dachshund

Changes To Watch For

Keep an eye out for different signs that your dog is slowing down. This will help you to know when to adjust the setup around your home and to reduce how much your old pup is exercising.

Appetite And Nutritional Requirements

With less exercise, your dog doesn't need as many calories, which means you need to adjust your pup's diet. If you opted to feed your Dachshund commercial dog food, make sure you change to a senior food. Senior food is designed for the changing dietary needs of older dogs, with fewer calories and more nutrients that the older dog's body needs.

If you make your Dachshund's food, talk to your vet and take the time to research how best to reduce calories without sacrificing taste. Your canine is going to need less fat in his food, so you may need to find something healthier that still has a lot of taste to supplement the types of foods you gave your Dachshund as a puppy or active adult dog.

Exercise

Since Dachshunds are so gregarious, they are going to be just as happy with extra attention from you as they were with exercise when they were younger. If you make fewer demands, decrease the number of walks, or in any way change the routine, your senior Dachshund will quickly adapt to the new program. You will need to make those changes based on your dog's ability, so it's up to you to adjust the schedule and keep your Dachshund happily active. Shorter, more frequent walks should take care of your Dachshund's exercise needs, as well as helping to break up your day a little more.

Your dog will enjoy napping as much as walking, especially if he gets to cuddle with you. Sleeping beside you while you watch television or as you yourself nap is pretty much all it takes to make your older Dachshund content, but he still needs to exercise.

The way your Dachshund slows down will probably be the hardest part of watching him age. You may notice that your Dachshund spends

Photo Courtesy
of Jackie Rivera

more time sniffing during walks, which could be a sign that your dog is tiring. It could also be his way of acknowledging that the steady walks are a thing of the past and so he is stopping to enjoy the little things more. Stopping to smell things may now give him the excitement that he used to get by walking farther.

While you should be watching for your dog to tire, he may also let you know. If he is walking slower, looking up at you, and flopping down, that could be his way of letting you know it's time to return home. If your canine can't manage long walks any longer, make the walks shorter and more numerous and spend more time romping around your yard or home with your buddy.

Aging And The Senses

Just like people, dogs' senses weaken as they get older. They won't hear things as well as they used to, they won't see things as clearly, and their sense of smell will weaken.

The following are some of the signs that your dog is losing at least one of his senses.

- It becomes easy to surprise or startle your dog. You need to be careful because this can make your Dachshund aggressive, a scary prospect even in old age. Do NOT sneak up on your old dog as this can be bad for both of you, and he deserves better than to be scared.

- Your dog may seem to ignore you because he is less responsive when you issue a command. If you have not had a problem before, your dog isn't being stubborn, he is likely losing his hearing.

- Cloudy eyes may be a sign of loss of sight, though it does not mean that your dog is blind.

If your dog seems to be "behaving badly," it is a sign that he is aging, not that he doesn't care or wants to rebel. Do not punish your older dog.

Adjust your schedule to meet your dog's changing abilities. Adjust his water bowl's height, refrain from rearranging rooms, and pet your dog more often. Make sure that his bed is as fluffy as when you first got it, or you can get him a new bed. Do make sure to put the bed on the ground if it was previously kept on furniture. He is probably nervous about losing his abilities, so it is up to you to comfort him.

Keeping Your Senior Dog Mentally Active

Just because your older Dachshund can't walk as far any longer doesn't mean that his brain isn't just as capable. In fact, the changes in his body will probably be frustrating for him, so you want to make sure he has plenty of other things to keep him active and happy. As he slows down physically, focus more on activities that are mentally stimulating. As long as your Dachshund has all of the basics down, you can teach him all kinds of low-impact tricks. At this point, training could be easier because your Dachshund has learned to focus better and he'll be happy to have something he can still do with you. New toys are another great way to help keep your dog's mind active. Be careful that the toys aren't too rough on your dog's older jaw and teeth. Games such as hide and seek will still be very much appreciated. Whether you hide toys or yourself, this can be a game that keeps your Dachshund guessing. There are also food balls, puzzles, and other games that focus on cognitive abilities. A quick search online will turn up a wealth of different toys meant to help intelligent dogs to keep from getting bored.

For a dog like the Dachshund, additional attention and more petting are more than enough to make them happy when they get older. They will want to cuddle up to you and just be loved. This will make your Dachshund as happy as possible, though you still want to make sure that your dog gets some physical and mental exercise regularly too. Even if your Dachshund's body has slowed down, his mind will tend to remain quite active.

Some senior dogs suffer from cognitive dysfunction (CCD) syndrome, a type of dementia. It is estimated that 85% of all cases of dementia in dogs go undiagnosed because of how difficult it is to pinpoint the problem. It manifests itself more as a problem of temperament.

If your dog begins to act differently, you should take him to the vet to see if he has CCD. While there really isn't any treatment for it, your vet can recommend things you can do to help your dog. Things like rearranging the rooms of your home are strongly discouraged as familiarity with his surroundings will help your dog feel more comfortable and will reduce stress as he loses his cognitive abilities. Mental stimulation will help to fight CCD, but you should plan to keep your dog mentally stimulated regardless of whether or not he exhibits symptoms of dementia.

Advantages To The Senior Years

The last years of your Dachshund's life can be just as enjoyable (if not more so) than the earlier stages since your dog has mellowed. All of those high-energy activities will give way to cuddles and relaxing. Having your pup just enjoy your company can be incredibly nice (just remember to keep up with some of his activity levels instead of getting too complacent with your Dachshund's newfound love of resting and relaxing).

Your Dachshund will continue to be a loving companion, interacting with you at every opportunity – that does not change with age. Your canine's limitations should dictate interactions and activities. If you are busy, make sure you schedule time with your Dachshund to do things that are within those limitations. It is just as easy to make an older Dachshund happy as it is with a young one, and it is easier on you since relaxing is more essential to your old friend.

Preparing To Say Goodbye

This is something that no pet parent wants to think about, but as you watch your Dachshund slow down, you will know that your time with your sweet pup is coming to an end. Some dogs tend to suddenly decline, making it very obvious when you need to start taking extra care of their aging bodies. They have trouble on smoother surfaces or can't walk nearly as far as they once did. It's certainly sad, but when it starts to happen, you know it is time to begin to prepare to say goodbye.

Some dogs can continue to live for years after they begin to slow down, but many dogs don't make it more than about a year or two. Sometimes dogs will lose their interest in eating, will have a stroke, or other problem that arises with little warning. Eventually, it will be time to say goodbye, whether at home or at the vet's. You need to be prepared, and that is exactly why you should be making the most of these last few years.

Talk to your family about how you will care for your dog over the last few years or months of his life. Many dogs will be perfectly happy, despite their limited abilities. Some may begin to have problems controlling their bowel movements, while others may have problems getting up from a prone position. There are solutions to all of these problems. It is key to remember that quality of life should be the primary consideration, and since your dog cannot tell you how he feels, you will have to take cues from your dog. If your dog still seems happy, there is no reason to euthanize him.

At this stage, your dog is probably very happy just sleeping near you for 18 hours a day. That is perfectly fine as long as he still gets excited about walking, eating, and being petted. The purpose of euthanasia is to reduce suffering, not to make things more convenient for yourself. This is what makes the decision so difficult, but your dog's behavior should be a fairly good indicator of how he is feeling. Here are some other things to watch to help you evaluate your dog's quality of life:

- Appetite
- Drinking
- Urinating and defecation
- Pain (noted by excessive panting)
- Stress levels
- Desire to be active or with family (if your dog wants to be alone most of the time, that is usually a sign that he is trying to be alone for the end)

Talk to your vet if your dog has a serious illness to determine what the best path forward is. They can provide the best information on the quality of your dog's life and how long your dog is likely to live with the disease or ailment.

If your dog gets to the point when you know that he is no longer happy, he can't move around, or he has a fatal illness, it is probably time to say goodbye. This is a decision that should be made as a family, always putting the dog's needs and quality of life first. If you decide it is time to say goodbye, determine who will be present at the end.

Once at the vet's office, if you have decided to euthanize the dog, you can make the last few minutes very happy by feeding your dog the things that he couldn't eat before. Things like chocolate and grapes can put a smile on his face for the remaining time he has.

You can also have your dog euthanized at home. If you decide to request a vet to come to your home, be prepared for additional charges for the home visit. You also need to determine where you want your dog to be, whether inside or outside, and in which room if you decide to do it inside.

Make sure at least one person he knows well is present so that your dog is not alone during the last few minutes of his life. You don't want your dog to die surrounded by strangers. The process is fairly peaceful, but your dog will probably be a little stressed. He will pass within a few minutes of the injection. Continue to talk to him as his brain will continue to work even after his eyes close.

Once your dog is gone, you need to determine what to do with the body.

- Cremation is one of the most common ways of taking care of the body. You can get an urn or request a container to scatter your dog's ashes over his favorite places. Make sure you don't dump his ashes in places where that is not permitted. Private cremation is more expensive than communal cremation, but it means that the only ashes you get are from your dog. Communal creation occurs when several pets are cremated together.

- Burial is the easiest method if you have your pet euthanized at home, but you need to check your local regulations to ensure that you can bury your dog at home because this is illegal in some places. You also need to consider the soil. If your yard is rocky or sandy, that will create problems with trying to bury your pet at home. Also, don't bury your pet in your yard if it is near wells that people use as a drinking source, or if it is near wetlands or waterways. Your dog's body can contaminate the water as it decays. You can also look into a pet cemetery if there is one in your area.

Grief And Healing

Dogs become members of our families, so their passing can be incredibly difficult. People go through all of the same emotions and feelings of loss with a dog as they do with close friends and family. The absence of that presence in your life is jarring, especially with such a loving, loyal dog like the Dachshund. It will feel weird not to have that little presence along behind you as you move around your home. Just as painful, your home is a constant reminder of the loss, and in the beginning you and your family will probably feel considerable grief. Saying goodbye is going to be difficult. Taking a couple of days off work is not a bad idea. While people who don't have dogs will say that your Dachshund was just a dog, you know better, and it is okay to feel the pain and to grieve like you would for any lost loved one.

215

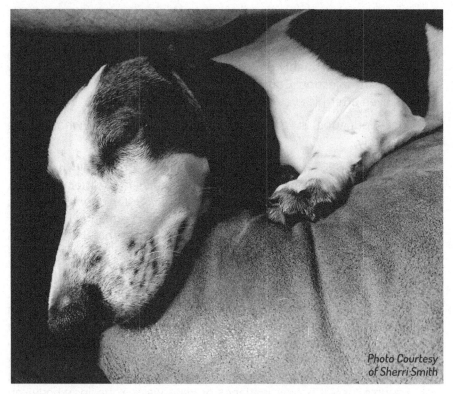

Photo Courtesy of Sherri Smith

Losing your Dachshund is also going to make a substantial change in your schedule. It will likely take a while to get accustomed to the way your day-to-day life has shifted. Fight the urge to go out and get a new dog because you almost certainly are not ready yet.

Everyone grieves differently, so you will need to allow yourself to grieve in a way that is healthy for you. Everyone in your family will feel the loss differently too, so let them feel it their own ways. Some people don't require much time, while others can feel the loss for months. There is no timetable, so don't try to force it on yourself or any member of your family.

Talk about how you would like to remember your pup, and make sure to listen. You can have a memorial for your lost pet, tell stories, and plant a tree in your dog's memory. If someone doesn't want to partici-pate, that is fine.

Try to return to your normal routine as much as possible if you have other pets. This can be both painful and helpful as your other pets will still need you just as much (especially other dogs that have also lost their companion).

If you find that grief is hindering your ability to function normally, seek professional help. If needed, you can go online to find support groups in your area to help you and your family, especially if this was your first dog. Sometimes it helps to talk about the loss so that you can start to heal.

Made in the USA
Coppell, TX
14 February 2024

29042628R00125